THE ART OF FLOWER ARRANGING

Marian Aaronson

Grower Books
London

Grower Books
50 Doughty Street, London WC1N 2LP

© Marian Aaronson 1970

First edition 1970
Second edition 1972
Third edition 1973
Reprinted 1975
Reprinted 1977
Fourth edition 1979
Reprinted 1980
Reprinted 1983

ISBN 0 901361 16 X

Library of Congress Catalog Card No: 77-579465

Printed in England by
Whitstable Litho Ltd., Whitstable, Kent

DEDICATION

To my finest critics—my two sons Michael and Robin

ACKNOWLEDGEMENTS

I would like to thank *Garden News* for the use of articles and photographs reproduced in this book. My warmest thanks to Ken Lauder for his never-failing patience, sympathetic help and superb photography. I am indebted to all my friends and readers everywhere who have encouraged me, to Eileen Poole for her constant co-operation and to my family for their splendid tolerance.

CONTENTS

INTRODUCTION

THIS BOOK has been designed with both the beginner and the more advanced student of flower arranging in mind. It covers the basic principles of designing, as well as some of the more progressive and creative aspects of arranging.

I have tried to make the more instructional section as interesting as possible, so as to encourage the individual's progress, from the beginning to the advanced stage. I believe that a true appreciation of the design principles, as the key to self-expression, is the best stimulus to progress along individual lines and the guiding influence in designing well, whatever type of expression is adopted.

The discipline involved in designing is a valuable training which fosters a deeper appreciation of all art forms, making it easier to see their basic similarities, since design is the common denominator in them all. In flower arranging, whether an arrangement is in the traditional, realistic or abstract manner, the factor that is constant is the designing principles.

Certain styles have become classic, like the traditional tri-linear Japanese arrangement, and the Western mass arrangement in flowing style—with its rich variety of colour and texture. Modern arrangements are now many and varied, with new styles that keep evolving from the old. As a progressive art form, flower arranging is embracing new ideas and attitudes compatible to contemporary living. In breaking away from conventional or traditional designing to find fresh ways of communicating ideas, the arranger experiments more freely with plant material. So designs to-day show more diversity, and no longer follow set patterns alone. They can vary from precise geometrical shapes to the free-form. Some are designed for a purely decorative effect, others are more expressive in character. Simplicity and clarity with a purity of form are typical of those designed for the streamlined modern home, where maximum effect is sought with a minimum of material, a few distinctive blooms replacing quantities of material. Though the clever massing of material for bold accents of texture and colour is also popular, this effect is often further accented by modern containers—with attractive glazings and colours and interesting form.

The progressive arranger no longer confines her scope for artistic effect to flowers alone, but realises the possibilities in all aspects of plant growth. 'Flower arrangement' is now taken in its widest context, to include all natural flora. Any facet can promote or play a distinctive role. Dried arrangements are no longer a substitute for the fresh; they have an important and accepted role in their own right, because of the added scope this medium gives for designing. Many arrangements are flowerless, dramatic pieces of wood sculpture. Stripped ivy, rattan cane twisted into different shapes, bleached honeysuckle, wisteria and vine are used with ingenuity; or shells, stones, fossils or an attractive accessory are used to promote the effectiveness of a sparse grouping.

Some designs depict nature realistically, others are a breakaway from the natural, and there are compositions with no subject beyond the design relationships.

All changes are not necessarily for the better, or always accept-able to the individual, since the personal idea of beauty is extremely variable. Every arranger sees things in a different way, and will have differing views. Cultivating a style compatible to oneself is the ideal—whatever the popular trend, and it is always possible to adapt the general to the personal point of view.

Some may view the advent of abstract trends in flower arrange-ment with dismay. To me, it is a new adventure in simplicity, and I delight in the freedom it offers to design to the limits of the media. These new horizons stimulate thought and promote our skill to give a new vision of the natural world.

In developing new ways of using plant material, and discovering further qualities in this, we extend the scope for designing with natural materials. The inclusion of non-floral objects, and the use of dyed plant material distresses many people. The criterion, as with everything else, is whether it adds to the artistic effect and furthers the beauty of one's work. The leveller should be discrimination and good taste, and of course, abiding by the fundamental principles of design.

Let flower arrangement be an art of natural and logical growth, with all that is good in the new, adding to, rather than replacing, the time-tested old. We now have a rich heritage to draw from, which should give the confidence and surety to move forward, with extensions that give stimulating new dimensions to flower arrangement as an art.

PART ONE

Chapter 1

THE FIRST STEPS

THE EASIEST way to begin anything is at the beginning. However tempting the thought of ignoring all the rules, and expressing oneself freely, the rudiments of arranging must be mastered first. It is only when the principles are fully understood that they can be adapted or modified to suit the more personal interpretation.

So the first few chapters deal with the basics. It is information and instruction that might help those of you who are comparatively new to flower arranging. This should help technically, and will also, I hope, inspire enthusiasm to progress in this rewarding and fulfilling art.

This does not mean, of course, you should make exact replicas of the examples given. Creating a flower arrangement is not like making a cake, using a well tried and tested recipe. It is a very personal expression reflecting the individual view and idea. This individuality is to be fostered and developed.

So whilst you can be guided by the arrangements and the ideas that are mine, it is important to cultivate your own ideas right from the beginning. With this as a basis, your arrangements are far less likely to become stereotyped and monotonous.

Make up your mind to be flexible and experimental—working with the imagination and being inventive is far more important than being technically perfect. Maybe the ideas will not come too readily to start with when you are feeling your way, but once confidence and enthusiasm are established, creative arranging becomes easier.

It is a good idea for the first few sessions to do nothing other than getting used to handling the plant material. This is particularly important at certain times of the year—as in early spring for instance, when forced flowers are so difficult to cope with. The heads are heavy and the stems are soft. Some are stiff and unyielding, and trying to arrange them in complicated patterns could prove very frustrating to a beginner.

It is better to start with something very simple, using a few

Fig. 1. Fine florist wire (cotton thread would also do) is wound around the daffodil stem to prevent splitting on the pins. The foliage, also tied around the stalk, gives added support to the soft stem. An ordinary and a well type pinholder are shown.

Fig. 2. Mechanics are more difficult here. I used sand to within a few inches of the top and added water. The iris stems are given extra support with two small sticks. The extra foliage also helps to stabilise their position.

flowers. Once you are familiar with the nature of your material, the way it behaves, its special attributes or its drawbacks, you can progress more smoothly, because you will have a much better idea of how to make the most of it.

In the arrangements in this chapter, I have simply grouped a few spring flowers to look as natural and graceful as possible. Study the way the daffodils are placed in Figs. 3 and 4, facing different ways, not all staring straight ahead. I have grouped a few of their own leaves around each stem for a more natural effect, and this helps to steady them on the pinholder also. Notice too, the angle at which

4

the flowers have been placed in the other two arrangements. A slight tilt of the stem keeps the head uplifted. This gives more sparkle to the design and a stronger impression of growth.

A few extra leaves, contrasting foliage, or the odd branch helps to soften the straight line and stiffness of the stems. Stones, water and additional placements add a little extra interest, and help to create a natural scene. A lot can be said with just a few flowers. Finding your own special way is the key to development.

The problem of mechanics and collecting the right equipment is dealt with in the next chapter.

Fig. 3. Two groupings on separate pinholders covered with pebbles suggest a natural scene. Branches are thin enough to fit easily between the pins.

Fig. 4. A pleasing arrangement of daffodils 'growing' in unison from the hollow of a container which takes a small pinholder.

Chapter 2

THE MECHANICS OF FLOWER ARRANGING

PERHAPS it isn't very exciting or inspiring to discuss the mechanics of arranging, but it is much more pleasurable to work on a firm and stable foundation, and the finished artistic effect is more assured with the right mechanics. Plant material can be stabilised in various ways depending on the nature of the material, the shape of the container and the particular effect required in the arrangement.

Today we have a good choice of mechanics to help us. One of the most popular is the pinholder. No serious arranger is without this effective prop, and it comes in various sizes and prices.

A 3 in. diameter one with pins set close together is a good initial buy. The larger pinholders with thick pins are excellent for branches and weighty material but are a little more expensive. There are square or rectangular ones for odd shaped containers, and well pinholders, with the pins set into a water container, are also useful. The holder can be given added stability with three small blobs of plasticine pressed to the back. Both container and holder must be quite dry to start with for perfect adhesion.

Don't ruin your pinholder by forcing the pins apart with heavy, wooded stems. Cut these at a slant, insert vertically, then ease carefully into the desired angle.

Hard wood which is dried is often impossible to anchor in this way, and there is a special driftwood holder for the job. This is a metal arm notched to hold florist wire and mounted on a small pinholder which fits into the larger one holding the plant material. It also has a small screw at the back which enables the branch or wood to be placed in different positions. Obtainable from Peter Harvey of Leeland Road, West Ealing.

Wire netting is a better answer in some types of container, like the tall earthenware jug in Fig. 6. The softer, 2 in. mesh wire is the easiest to handle. Here, a long narrow piece was loosely crumpled and pushed to within a couple of inches of the bottom of

Fig. 5. An attractive branch
anchored in a large pin-
holder. Bottom of the stem
is cut on a slant.

Fig. 6. Mechanics for a tall, narrow container with a sparse line arrangement. Pieces of loose wire are twisted around the stems for extra support.

Fig. 6a. A few foliage sprays hide the wire without spoiling the line. The more wire you use, the more you have to cover.

the container. A little left above the rim of the jug gives anchorage
and saves the whole piece being pushed down as the stems go in.

Don't use too much wire, and ease the stems between the holes,
which should be as evenly spaced as possible so that there are no
hard, unresisting areas to get through. This type of container and
mechanics is a little difficult to master at first, so practise on the
easier, pinholder mechanics to start with, then gradually use these
more tricky but attractive vases.

When using a candlestick or a flower holder similar to the
cherub container in Fig. 7, water-retaining foam such as Oasis or
Stemfix is ideal. The container can be moved without fear of

Fig. 7. The mechanics suited
to a soft, flowing design.
The candle cup fits into an
opening like a candle stick.

spilling water, and it is easy to put in the stems at the desired angle. It is especially useful for thin, fine stems like freesia. An Oasis holder anchors the block which was soaked before insertion in the candle cup holder. The foam must be saturated with extra water when necessary.

Stemfix, which was previously made in white only, is now obtainable in green too, and can be bought in large or small blocks. For dried stems, florists' clay, sold in blocks, can be used, or a firm plastic foam called Dri-hold.

You will probably collect containers as you go along. It is a mistake to rush into buying too many until you are sure which type best suits your style. Three of a similar type to those shown in this chapter would do to start with—as each would be an exercise in different mechanics. Perhaps a candlestick instead of the cherub, a flat Denby dish and an attractive jug or tall jar. Subdued earthy colours and matt textures are easier to use and are usually more harmonious with the plant material than very shiny highly coloured surfaces.

Chapter 3

CONDITIONING OF PLANT MATERIAL

THE LIFE of cut flowers is a short one, but there are one or two things that can be done to preserve it for as long as possible, so that arrangements which have taken time, thought and money to assemble, give maximum returns.

A fresh looking, crisp arrangement is a refreshing sight, even when the design is perhaps not perfect. Sad, droopy flowers, even in the most intriguing creation, look only pathetic.

The answer is to make sure that the rate of transpiration (evaporation of water) does not exceed the amount of water entering the stem and that the conducting vessels do not become clogged with bacteria.

When a stem is cut the cells start to close up. So the sooner the flower or leaf is in water the better. Garden material can be put straight into water. A bucket may not be as artistic as a basket or tray, but it is better for the flowers. The best time for cutting is early morning or after sundown—never in the heat of the day. I have found this immediate placing in water prevents most plants from wilting. Some material is notoriously difficult to condition though, and with these, absorption can be boosted by boiling or burning the stem ends for about 20 to 30 seconds. This disperses any air bubbles that have formed, preventing water travelling up the stem. It also breaks down the layer of non-porous material which forms over some cut stems. Re-cutting stems under water helps to prevent an air lock forming.

Florists' flowers need re-cutting before being plunged into deep water for several hours, preferably over-night. All plant material needs this long pre-arrangement draught; they can then survive on moderate drinking. If flowers are put in full sunlight or a very hot room, all the conditioning in the world will not do much to prolong their lives.

Foliage absorbs water through its surface, as well as its stem.

Leafy branches and leaves, except grey woolly ones, should be submerged in water for several hours. It is better to remove some of the leaves from flowering shrubs, as they will drink more greedily and at the expense of the flower, since their rate of transpiration will be faster. Items like lilac, philadelphus and *Virburnum opulus* (guelder rose) are best defoliated completely. Woody stems need the last inch or two crushed, otherwise the flower head will droop before water reaches it.

The white portion from the stem tips of bulbous flowers should be cut as these drink only through the green portion. Rinse the stem ends of daffodils with luke-warm water to remove the sticky substance they exude. Tulips are best wrapped up in newspaper to keep the stems straight. After their initial deep drink, bulb flowers thrive happily in shallow water.

Euphorbias and plants giving off a milky sap when cut should have the stem tips singed or placed in boiling water for ten seconds or so. It is a good idea to have a little sand to dip the ends into when

Fig. 8. The gerberas opposite were wrapped in tissue paper and the stems placed in a few inches of hot (not boiling) water, then left until the water was cold. Foliage is of *Helleborus corsicus.*

Fig. 9. Long lasting foliage of bergenia, *Mahonia aquifolium* and euonymus. The sansevieria are lifted out of the water slightly by a false stem. They would rot in deep water.

Fig. 10. Practical durable leaves—clivia, fatsia, *Senecio greyii*, aspidistra and *Arum italicum.*

13

cutting from the garden. The hollow stems of lupins and delphiniums can be filled with water and plugged with cotton wool before their long drink.

Wilting flowers can be revived by warm or hot water—the stronger the stem the hotter the water can be. Protect the flower heads from steam with tissue paper and leave until the water is cold. It is amazing how some really limp flowers perk up with this treatment. Gerberas and anemones are particularly responsive. To discourage bacteria, see that all containers are clean to start with. Rinse the pinholder well, and cut off all leaves below water level. A coffee spoonful of bleach added to the water helps to keep it pure.

Have a little water in the container when arranging to prevent the stems drying out. Top up with warm water. Buy or cut the freshest possible flowers. Examine the foliage of florists' flowers— it should be crisp and a good colour.

These are general hints. Flowers are really quite like people; they can be temperamental—some days they behave well, at other times they are a trifle difficult. Some are thirsty creatures, others more restrained in drinking habits. A few, like violets, hydrangeas and some of the hellebores, like drinking through their petals. In time one gets to know their little idiosyncracies and how to cope with them.

Chapter 4

WHY DESIGN?

HAVING decided on the most suitable type of mechanics and conditioned the plant material, the next step is to construct the arrangement. This is the rewarding, interesting part, and you will naturally want the result to be as pleasing as possible. You should also aim for the maximum creative satisfaction from the exercise itself.

We know it is possible to get quite attractive effects sometimes, by merely placing the items in a vase, without following any arranging principles. This might be due to the charming colours used, or the beauty of the flowers themselves. Why, then, do we bother to design an arrangement?

It is that, all too often, haphazard placements result in bunchy, confused groupings lacking order and unity. Besides, this is not a very challenging way of arranging. It is much more stimulating to think of every arrangement as something you compose. Each separate part is important by itself, but each should be considered and used in relation to the whole, so that the overall effect is of a pleasing, integrated whole.

In a well designed flower arrangement, the eye can move rhythmically throughout. There is no jarring note, and, one has the impression of a balanced unified whole, rather than a collection of separate items. It is like looking at a well-planned house of pleasing pattern. One sees the overall unified building, not a collection of doors, windows and chimneys. We plan and arrange our living room so that it has orderly appeal, is well balanced with emphasis where needed, and a pleasing continuity throughout.

Clearly then we plan, organise or design, because it makes the composition easier to look at, holds our attention longer and is aesthetically more satisfying.

How do we go about this process? We design by following certain principles, which are basic to all art. They are balance, scale, proportion, rhythm, contrast, variety and dominance.

As fundamentals these principles have remained unchanged over

the centuries but their application can be infinitely varied. You will find, as you progress, that each can be modified to suit the particular expression, or the specific effect required. They are, therefore, not rigid laws that restrict creativity. When fully understood, these can be made to work for, not against you, as they can guide the designer to the most effective ways of communicating ideas and impressions.

It is important to see it this way, so as not to become obsessed by design, since design itself is not the ultimate aim, merely the means to an end. Over-concern with rules can be crippling, and result in monotonous, repetitive compositions.

Some schools of thought in art reject the teaching of any principles before the student is confronted with paper and pencil, oil

Fig. 11. An informal design. There is an asymmetrical balance between the wood and the flowers and leaves. Lilies follow the line of the driftwood for rhythm and continuity, giving a well integrated composition.

Fig. 12. A formal design. Arrangement is pleasantly proportionate to container and bases. Though a mass, there is a planned relationship of spaces and solids. Items have been grouped, not dotted haphazardly. This gives rhythm and continuity.

and canvas or whatever medium used. The pupil starts with an open mind, uninhibited by theories or another's point of view.

But unless one has a natural flair for design, or a very highly developed artistic appreciation, this can be rather bewildering. Most beginners feel the need of some basis on which to begin. This helps pull together thoughts and actions. It acts as a stabiliser and gives confidence.

Progressively, the basic principles will be applied less consciously. Your more trained eye and developing aesthetic sense will tell you when anything in the arrangement is top heavy, unbalanced or out of harmony. You will still abide by natural laws in designing, but, with experience, learn to adapt them to different requirements.

Chapter 5

BALANCE

AS MENTIONED in the last chapter, a good design conforms to all the basic principles. Each is really inter-related, and correctly applied, works one for the other. It is confusing however, to consider these all at once in an arrangement, and easier to analyse them separately.

We begin with three principles that are closely allied—namely, balance, scale and proportion.

Balance is generally thought of in terms of weight, and the force of gravity. When we stand upright, weight is distributed equally on either side of the body. If we walk, run or climb a tree, the distribution of this weight is shifted to maintain equilibrium. This kind of balance is necessary for our safety and comfort.

In nature, plant material is thicker at the base when it grows from the soil. In a bloom spike, the largest form is generally at the base, with size diminishing gradually to the tip. The trunk of a tree is thicker than the branches. This gives a pleasing impression of stability.

Balance plays an important role in our reactions to art also. The eye is offended and our aesthetic sense disturbed by anything which looks unbalanced or unstable. We demand the same feeling of stability in an artistic creation.

To ensure this the designer must respect the laws of balance. This, in the visual arts like painting and flower arranging, is the visual weight relationship. In this instance, when a stem is called heavy or light, we mean that it looks light or heavy. In a flower arrangement, it is the visual weight of the plant material, container, base, accessories and so on, that must be considered and their distribution planned for a well balanced composition.

Everything used in an arrangement affects its balance. Every colour, form, line and texture must be considered in terms of its visual weight factor, and its effect on the overall balance of the design. In traditional, conventional arranging we follow nature's technique by placing items with the greater visual weight—the largest forms, the strongest colours, the thickest lines—low in the

design. With the visually lighter, paler colours, smaller forms, thinner lines, at the top and to the outside of the design.

In the figurine composition in Fig. 13, you will notice that the denser, thicker and darker area is at the centre, with the light, sparser material at the top. In the gladioli grouping also—Fig. 14—the thinner, pointed forms make the outline of the design, with the larger, heavier forms at the base.

If you draw an imaginary line vertically through the central axis of both these arrangements, you will notice that the items differ in type but have equal visual weight for balance. In the one, the darker leaves and the figurine balance the taller branch and greater profusion of blossom on the other side. In the second grouping, the considerable visual weight of the blackened branch and darker portion of the container is compensated by the additional black base and the spears of foliage on the opposite side.

This balance of form and colour with dissimilar items is known as asymmetrical balance, and is usually more interesting and

Fig. 13. Pink and white cherry blossom on the one side is balanced by a figurine of the same colour on the other side of the centre line. The base gives stability to the perpendicular line.

20

subtler than balance with identical objects. This more forceful asymmetric balance is more noticeable perhaps in Fig. 15, where line is balanced by solid forms. Here the weight of the driftwood is countered by two round bases. The placement of the strongest colour (white) also stabilises the design.

Notice, though, that the flowers are lifted slightly off the base, so as to maintain the vigorous movement of the design. Larger items or a thickly packed area placed directly on the base, or the edge of the container, can reduce the movement of the design or even make the lower half of the arrangement appear too heavy, whereas the space underneath allows the eye to move freely through the pattern.

Good proportioning and scaling of the items used also affects the balance of an arrangement, but this will be dealt with fully in the next chapter.

Fig. 14. A vertical line of gladioli is made more interesting by a blackened branch balanced by a base of the same colour on the opposite side.

Fig. 15. A line arrangement with interesting balance maintained without making the design static.

Chapter 6

PROPORTION AND SCAL

PROPORTION and scale are two closely allied principles and their use in arrangements affects the beauty and unity of the design.

Proportion is the ratio of one area or one part of a structure to another and to the whole. Harmonious proportions can be created by adjusting the size of one area to another.

Scale is the size relationship of the separate units of a structure to each other, and to the whole. Pleasing scale exists when units which are reasonably harmonious in size are used together.

Flower arrangers do not necessarily approach their art in a mathematical way by designing their arrangements with the aid of ruler and compass. They usually rely more on intuition and artistic judgement. We might indeed assume that if a thing feels or looks right, it usually is! Yet on analysis the basic mathematics behind it all can be traced though these have not necessarily been applied consciously. A good framework is the basis of a good arrangement and this framework is made out of simple shapes like triangles and circles. Out of geometry in fact.

It is believed that the ancient Egyptians were the first to apply mathematics in art. They discovered many satisfying proportions, among them the Golden Section, or the Golden Proportion, which was used as a basis of beauty in their buildings, and art. Eudoxos, a Greek mathematician, worked out the formula of the Golden Proportion which Greek painters, potters, sculptors and above all, architects, used as a basis to make many wonderful designs and shapes. That superlative piece of architecture, the Parthenon in Athens, was so exquisitely proportioned, with each part so sensitively related to the whole, that it is still considered the most beautiful and harmonious building ever created.

|————————————————————|——————————|
A   B   C

The Golden Section is the division of a line in such a way that the smaller part is in the same proportion to the greater part as

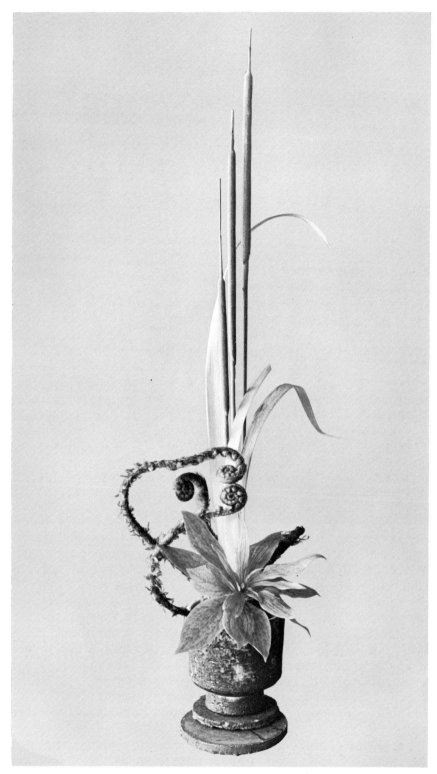

Fig. 16. Here the height of the light pointed material is more than the customary $1\frac{1}{2}$ times the height of the container. This gives added emphasis to the vertical line.

23

that greater part is to the whole, like this: BC is to AB as AB is to AC. The Golden Section of the line is at B. Its aesthetic appeal lies in a proportion of elements that is neither too equal nor too contrasting, but an ideal proportion.

All this would seem a long way from flower arrangement, yet here too, we aim at relating part to whole in proportions that are pleasing and beautiful. In the diagram AB is roughly one and a half times BC. This is the familiar accepted guide which flower arrangers use in proportioning plant material to container. It is a good plan to start the arrangement using this ratio, and to re-examine the effect on completion. In many instances it will still be the right proportion, but adjustments will be necessary at other times.

To achieve satisfying proportions between plant material and container, and good proportions of line, form, texture, colour and

Fig. 17. A conventionally proportioned, traditional grouping with the plant materials in harmonious scale to each other and to the container.

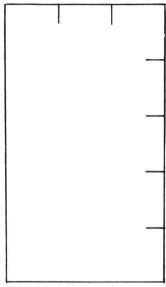

The Golden Mean

space in the design, many things must be given consideration: the nature of the plant material, the design and type of interpretation, size and shape of container and the arrangement's setting.

When set in a niche, the arrangement naturally must be proportionate to its dimensions. The majority of flower show niches are rectangular rather than square. The proportions here conform to the 'Greek Oblong', determined by the Golden Mean—that is, a rectangle with sides in the ratio of 2:3 or 3:5. Again, width and length are neither too equal nor too different, and is aesthetically more satisfying than equal proportions.

Correct scale also enhances an arrangement. Harmony depends on using items of good size relationship, i.e. of leaf to flower, flower to branch or wood, plant material to container, or accessories, and so on. When items of disparate sizes are used together, it is generally necessary to use an intermediate size as a transition.

Fig. 18. Careful selection means that the accessories are neither too large nor too small for their placement in this design.

25

Chapter 7

CONTRAST, VARIETY AND UNITY

IT IS VARIETY that gives life its savour, since it is through contrast that we are made aware of differences. Without night, we could not appreciate day, calm without storm, the heat of summer without the cold of winter. The value of each is emphasised by contrast with its opposite.

Nature is never monotonous. Can you think of a single natural object that does not show variety? Flowers, insects, birds, trees and animals have a multitude of diverse parts. There is variety in the separate elements of mountains, meadows, rivers and sky in the overall landscape. Yet all these different parts are put together, for one whole, unified effect. Nature combines them so that they merge their separate identities.

This is the aim of the artist also—to use the two principles of variety and unity, in such a way that they complement and supplement each other, so that they inter-act and balance one another in a satisfying manner. The 'theme and variations' in the musical form has the variety of tempo, rhythm and tone, but all are combined into one main theme, the sounds and silences are integrated for one total effect.

In flower arranging too, variety and contrast are necessary to prevent monotony. The eye soon becomes bored with sameness. A well-organised, meticulous flower arrangement with no contrasting element present lacks the spark needed to bring the design to life. It lacks vitality, and fails to hold our attention for long. Without the relief that contrast brings there is no unity, since there is no focus to hold our attention, which is the first step towards appreciating whatever we look at.

A flower arrangement using all pointed forms, or all shiny textures would give no lasting satisfaction. But with the contrast of a round or oval form, the beauty of the pointed material is enhanced. A rough texture would emphasise the qualities of the

Fig. 19. Sharp contrasts of line; the exciting zig-zag of the clipped iris leaves is made more emphatic by the gentle circular movement of reeds and curled leaves. Unity is maintained through continuity of line and form in plant material and container.

27

shiny surfaces; a dominant line can often be made more forceful
by the opposition of a subordinate, contrasting one (see the iris
arrangement in Fig. 19). Bright colour can be intensified through
contrast with a duller hue. A white flower appears whiter against a
dark background. Variety of hue and texture, to create light and
shadow adds depth and movement as in the lily arrangement in
Fig. 20.

Much depends on the way in which variety is organised. So
often, in modern and abstract arrangements, the impact of the
design depends on sharp contrasts with no transitional items to
reduce the effect—like dramatic complementary colour harmonies,
or sharp differences of line, form or texture.

Subtle differences are more restful. Here the use of an intermediate unit acts as a modifier. As, for instance, smaller florets of

leaves, between a stark branch and a large round form. Analogous colour schemes are harmonious and easy to look at; though here too, a small touch of complementary colouring can liven up the design.

But, as in nature, variety gives more lasting pleasure when the separate units merge, to give a single impression, a unified whole. Too many contrasting elements placed in an unco-ordinated manner are hard to 'take in' and endanger unity.

All the contrasting elements, the diversity of materials, the different forms, colours, texture, lines of movement and the spatial organisation should be balanced and rhythmically related to give a pleasant continuity throughout. Even in the most abstract design—or the most dramatic grouping—this is important. In this way, variety works for unity.

Fig. 21. There are interesting contrasts of colour and texture here, but it is variety of form in solids and spaces that pulls together the separate items into a unified whole.

Chapter 8

RHYTHM

MUCH OF THE appeal of a flower arrangement lies in its rhythmical quality. This is the movement created by a series of accents and pauses, of motion and rest, as in the motion of walking and in the rise and fall of waves. Each area of pause directs the eye to move on to the next pause, and then the next one, and so on until the whole design has been encompassed.

This sequence of continuity gives order and harmony and at the same time vitalises the design, whereas a flower arrangement lacking the co-ordination of its separate parts is static and stilted.

Movement can be organised in several ways, the most obvious by repeating certain factors. This may be of line, form, colour or texture. In Fig. 23 rhythm is achieved by repetition of circular forms. This starts with the shape of the base, is continued in the container, and repeated again in the round flowers. This draws the eye upward in a spiralling movement. In Fig. 24 also, line and colour is continued from accessories to base, to plant material in easy sequence.

These repeated factors, then, generate the main movement of these designs—they unify the parts to give a smooth continuity throughout the arrangement. But the repetition of an unchanging rhythm can become monotonous, like the tick of a clock. The eye continues in the same directed movement until it is re-directed by another stimulus.

A certain variation is needed to maintain interest. Within the major rhythm, minor rhythms can be created through contrast, to sustain the vitality of the design and our continuing attention. These subordinate, contrasting movements create their own rhythms within the major or dominant movement of each arrangement. In all three examples in this chapter the eye is drawn rhythmically from front to rear, from side to side, and from below upwards without being held too long in any one area. This makes the design more lively and buoyant; unlike one made static or overpowered by a heavy, mis-used 'focal point'!

Fig. 22. Iris spears trimmed into dramatic angles spiral in an ascending line for a beautifully rhythmic pattern.

30

Fig. 23. Spider chrysanths and bulrushes in an ascending spiralling rhythm which is smooth and restful.

Movement can be of varying tempo. Some rhythms are sharp and staccato, others lazy and langorous, swift or exciting. The specific nature of the rhythm and the differing feelings it produces may be used to convey a restless mood, peace, serenity or gaiety. Its expressiveness can help to communicate the particular idea, emotion or atmosphere the arranger wishes to interpret.

Fig. 24. An exciting rhythm created with a variety of directional movements.

33

Fig. 25. The dominance of
the strelitzia flowers is both
emphasised and balanced by
the other elements.

34

Chapter 9

DOMINANCE

THE PRINCIPLE of dominance is perhaps best described as giving the proper emphasis to the parts and to the whole in design. It is a process of differentiating the more important from the less important and is as basic to art as it is to all life's activities.

Emphasis in design serves us in many ways. When some things are stressed and others minimised, interest is captured, whereas a design where everything is of equal importance, is either too confusing or too monotonous to hold attention for long.

Imagine a flower arrangement where all the colours are equally bright, all the items the same size, or even worse, all the surfaces fussy and distracting. There would be no areas of rest or pause, no dominance to give unity. Holding and releasing attention is fundamental to art.

Viewing is easier when one basic idea is stressed. Dominance therefore, helps to bring a sense of order. Also when the highlights are limited to a number appropriate to the particular situation or effect required, the more important or dominant feature is emphasised and gains in effect.

Emphasis in design is achieved in several ways—often one item is dominant enough to direct the choice of the remaining items. Care must be taken though in case any single item becomes conspicuously dominant. In a good composition we are not conscious of one focal point, but of a number of areas of interest—some of higher, some of lesser interest, areas of motion and areas of rest. It is only when they are well balanced and integrated that one whole total effect is achieved.

In the strelitzia arrangement here—Fig. 25—it is the striking shapes and bright colours of the flowers that command most attention. But so that the eye is not held too rigidly in one spot, a balanced relationship is necessary between them and the rest of the composition. In the other areas of interest here, the wood complements the line of the flowers, the plain, strap-like leaves provide contrast in form and the container balances their size. This

integration of the separate elements carries the eye at varying tempo through the design, and we see the arrangement as a whole.

Bold shapes and brilliant colours are more noticeable than neutral ones; size is also important, as is the unusual or the unexpected. We pay attention to something that is different. The amount of emphasis will, of course, depend on the needs of the design. In Fig. 26 it is the exciting line and the spaces created by the branch that is the dominant feature. But we notice the other items also, the attractive colour and texture of the flowers and the pleasing shape of the container. These give variety to the interest areas and, at the same time, sustain the main theme by furthering the strong spatial interest of the design. The line of the flowers accents the upward thrust of the branch and the container 'moves' in an ascending, circular motion.

Again, in Fig. 27, the first thing we notice is the forceful line of the branches and the space they enclose. But the eye is urged along by rhythmic repetition to the line of the base, and back again to the outline, pausing on its way at the other areas of interest.

There is a stimulating harmony in the variety of texture, form and colour in container, flowers and leaves. All are integrated for an ever-changing, varied line of movement and emphasis.

Fig. 26. The powerful movement of the branch is strengthened by the line of the flowers and container.

36

Fig. 27. The form of this arrangement is made of different integrated elements that create similar and contrasting rhythms.

37

Chapter 10

THE ELEMENTS OF DESIGN

FORM, LINE, space, texture, and colour are the elements which artists and designers in the graphic arts use to communicate ideas and meaning, just as words and sounds are used in the time arts of music and poetry. Like the principles of design they are all inter-related, but for clarification they will be discussed separately. We will start with line.

Line is a powerful design element, and is used both as a unit of construction and of expression in art. In flower arrangement, lines are needed to create a path of motion that will take the eye smoothly through the structure of the design. Handled in a certain way, almost any material can be made to do this, but the forms and structure of certain plants lend themselves more readily than others. Like the iris spears, pampas grass, bare twig, and the fine stems of ivy in Figs. 28 to 31, the eye moves smoothly along their form, and because of this, they are often referred to as line material. Flowers like delphinium, larkspur and gladiolus, are other examples.

You will also see that the way the round flowers in Fig. 28 have been placed, creates a series of movements, as the eye is drawn from one to the other; the motion is the line. In Fig. 29 where they are bunched together more, they have lost their individual pull.

The way the line of material is organised, determines the main movement of the design. In Fig. 30, the dominant line of the arrangement as a whole is upward or vertical. In Fig. 31, movement is in a diagonal path, whilst the eye moves in a semi-circular line in Fig. 28.

Other movements of secondary importance can give variety of course—as in Fig. 30, where the vertical line is made a little more interesting with a slightly advancing movement in the loop of willow. The line of the container here stresses the line of the arrangement. Very often, a vertical arrangement is made on a horizontal base. This creates a rather different rhythm, as the

Fig. 28. A curved line is easy on the eye.

39

horizontal line modifies the upward movement of the arrangement, whereas all the units moving in the same direction strengthens the dominant motion.

Crossing and changing lines can give vigour and sparkle to the design. In modern work we are no longer slaves to the old adage of never crossing stems. But this must be done properly, and only when it adds to the attractiveness of the design. Note how the line of the twigs crossing the vertical pampas in Fig. 29 increases the depth and adds to the spatial interest of the design. The arrangement would indeed be quite flat and lifeless without this. It also improves the balance and rhythm of the design. You will find many more examples of this principle throughout the book.

Variations in line are clearly endless. A line can move quickly or slowly, smoothly or jerkily. Study the varying tempo in the examples in this chapter, and also the variety of line, from thick, thin, straight, curved, visible or invisible. The invisible are lines supplied by the eye in recording separate items. Notice how easily the eye moves from the dark twigs to the outline of the dark base in Fig. 29.

Fig. 29. Interesting lines that combine for a rhythmical pattern.

40

Fig. 30. A vertical movement that might be an interpretation of 'spring'.

41

The rhythmic, vital quality of line makes it an expressive element in design. The arranger may convey many moods, and suggest different ideas through the direction and quality of line. Vertical lines which remind us of straight tree trunks or church spires have the same, uplifting effect suggesting dignity and aspiration. Again the association of a horizontal line with that of the horizon, or open plains, or the sea, induces a feeling of peace and calm. Zig-zag lines are more active, like lightning flashes, diagonal lines can also convey fast movement. Curving lines have a more soothing influence, like those of gently meandering rivers. Lines that spiral upwards suggest growth and vigour, or joy or gaiety. Other factors in the design will naturally affect the overall impression, and may modify the general effect. For instance, a horizontal can be restless and disquieting if other factors strongly suggest this.

Handled expertly, line is an element of astonishing beauty. The artist of the East has been aware of this for centuries, and has made magical use of it. The controlled line-pattern of the traditional Japanese flower arrangement is incomparable in its simplicity and superb restraint. Now, line is often the dominant feature in modern western arrangements too. Plant material is frequently kept to the minimum, and distributed so as to fully reveal the beauty of line.

Fig. 31. Thin nervous lines moving diagonally for a lively arrangement suggesting a windswept theme.

42

Chapter 11

TEXTURE

OF ALL THE design elements, texture is the one most directly concerned with sense of touch. It is the tangible surface quality of an object. Every material has texture which produces varying sensations when touched. This, in designing terms, is known as its tactile value. When we buy clothes or furnishing fabrics, it is instinctive to touch them, to feel their quality. The sense of touch helps in making a selection.

The flower arranger too, uses texture to enhance an arrangement. In this sphere, as in a painting, our appreciation is visual. We know, without actually touching and through association with the sense of touch, what the various surfaces feel like, and enjoy their various qualities by looking at them. Even textures which are repellent to the touch, like gorse, thistle, chestnut burrs and teasles are attractive to look at.

In plant material, the surface appearance is determined by the structure and formation of the plant tissues, which can vary from smooth to coarse, hard to soft, shining to dull, tough to fragile—with many other variations like prickly, furry, hairy, woolly, downy, velvety, woody, leathery, silky, satiny and so on. The flower arranger has a wonderfully varied selection of textures, found in nature. A soft-velvety rose petal, glossy camellia leaves, woolly rosettes of verbascum, satiny smooth driftwood and rough crinkly bark, to name but a few. Some plants have more than one texture in their structure. Cow parsley is rough, lacey and fragile. Onopordon leaves are woolly, matt, and prickly. Laurel leaves are glossy and leathery.

These qualities, found in plants, and also in containers, drape and accessories, the arranger uses to enhance, and increase interest in, the design. Using texture well is as important as choosing the right colours, because the way texture is distributed in an arrangement will affect its balance, rhythm, and force of the design, just as with colour distribution.

Glossy surfaces are very eye-catching, so they should be placed

Fig. 32. A composition of dried and preserved plant material in shades, tints and tones of brown with interesting textures.

Fig. 33. The dominant rough texture of the flowers is contrasted by the smooth driftwood and the container.

where they will not upset the balance of the design. Very shiny containers or accessories can be distracting for this reason. Dull, matt surfaces are generally easier to use in large quantities. The contrast of shiny against dull, rough with smooth, can add to the interest of the design, since the quality of each is stressed and enhanced by their differences. The shiny, smooth vase in Fig. 32 sets off the coarse, dull texture of the monkey-puzzle and wild clematis. The smoothness of the driftwood in Fig. 33 enhances the rough texture of the chrysanthemums.

The textural quality of an item is affected by lighting. A rough surface will be intensified in shadow. In full light these shadows will disappear. Turning plants to different planes will create a play of light-and-shade effect, which enhances the rhythm of the design.

In Fig. 34 you will notice how much stronger the textural effect is in the lower leaf, which is in half-shadow, than the one above it in direct light. Some textures appear to advance, others to recede. This can add an illusion of space in the arrangement. Smooth, dull surfaces seem to recede into space, shiny and rough ones to move forward.

Apart from these contributions, texture can also add to the expressiveness of the design and so can help interpretation. Its different qualities are associated with different things or ideas. Roughness suggests strength or masculinity, fine textures something more delicate and feminine, prickly, bristly surfaces remind one more of viciousness or anger, whilst satiny, silky textures are more readily associated with sophistication.

Fig. 34. A variety of texture in an all-foliage arrangement.

Chapter 12

SPACE

THE PATTERN of an arrangement is made up of solids and spaces —the plant material and the areas in between. The proportion of the solid areas to the empty ones determines the nature and character of the pattern—its openness or solidity. In the mass arrangement of old, the tendency was to pack flowers close together and few spaces were left unfilled. This often resulted in lavish, splendid displays, rich in texture and colour, but lacking movement and vitality.

Today's arranger, however, is fully aware of the value and importance of space in enhancing a design. The pattern of distinctive modern styles clearly demonstrates the beauty of space; the spatial pattern is planned with as much thought and care as texture, form or colour. Even the mass arrangement today has a more open silhouette, with a more pleasing ratio of spaces to solids than before. In the small, traditional type grouping here (Fig. 35), each flower is sufficiently isolated to reveal its form and beauty fully, and planned spacing in the outline gives a livelier silhouette.

But by comparison, space plays a much more dynamic and important role in the three modern arrangements in this chapter. Here, space is a living force, vitalising the design. Without this attention to the spatial pattern, the significance of the solid items would be greatly reduced. Now, each is sharply defined and the beauty of separate items can be fully appreciated. Notice how the spaces balance the solids. This is less monotonous than solid balancing solid. In Fig. 36, the large area of space between the top of the gladiolus and the left hand edge of the container balances the greater number of solid items on the other side. The eye-catching enclosed space in Fig. 37 supports the weight of the container creating an interesting balance with contrast. Clearly, areas of space used positively can adequately balance items of considerable visual weight.

Spaces in a pattern are more interesting when irregular. Study the space shapes in the illustrations and notice how monotony is

Fig. 35. An interesting pattern of form and space in a slightly fuller arrangement.

46

Fig. 36. Expressing beauty of space. Here full emphasis is given to line and form; note how the areas of space balance the solid elements.

48

Fig. 37. A dynamic area of enclosed space to balance the solid items.

49

avoided through variety. The spaces become as interesting as the solid items. The container in each arrangement plays its part in the spatial interest. In Fig. 36, you will see how the space left between the last placements and the rim of the container increases movement and spatial beauty also. This lifts the design up into space.

Illusionary space can be created in a design to give added depth and movement. The three iris spears in Fig. 36, set in a diagonal plane, appear to move far back into the distance. In the same arrangement you will see by the placement of the two round leaves, how one urges the eye to move upwards and backwards into space, the other moving it forward and outward. Here too, the gladioli, arranged to face in different directions, increase the depth appearance. Spatial illusion is created in Fig. 37 where light and dark values very noticeably advance and recede, the dark drawing the eye inwards, the light pushing it outwards. Without this push and pull effect, designs of this nature might assume a rather flat appearance.

Crossing lines, and overlapping planes also create a feeling of depth—this we witnessed in arrangements in Chapter 10. Texture too, can help to give illusionary space. Rough textures appear to advance, smooth ones to recede. This can be seen in the arrangements featuring texture in Chapter 11. Mass arrangements depend a great deal on illusionary space. Careful grouping of advancing and receding lines, and of texture is needed to prevent a confused, indiscernible mass.

Apart from the space within the design which we have just studied, the relationship between the arrangement and the area in which it is created must be considered. This may be a niche, or a setting in a room in the home, or any building.

The arranger, unlike the painter on a two-dimensional surface, works in a volume of space, having the dimensions of height, width and depth, and with three-dimensional material. The size of the volume which the arrangement defines will depend on the relative factors such as the dimensions of the room, the furniture and so on—or on the size of the niche, where the boundaries are more clearly defined. This relationship of the arrangement to the larger space involved is an important consideration in enhancing the composition. This should be remembered at the start, with the first placements which will determine the length, width, and depth of the arrangement.

The arranger should take advantage of the possibilities offered by working in three-dimensional space. Consider, and work around the composition, not in a shallow frontal framework. In this way you will come to place the material so that it makes the most stimulating use of space.

Chapter 13

FORM

FORM, AS applied to design, has two different meanings which can be confusing. There is form, referring to the total organisation of the design; and form as an element meaning shape or structure. The form of a flower arrangement in the context of the first meaning is the complete expression, the sum total of all that has gone into its organisation. This form will vary with style and the intent of the arranger.

Shape on the other hand, is an element, along with line, texture, space and colour, that the designer uses to portray ideas. Form, too, is expressive, so the arranger selects the form most suitable in conveying the theme or the particular effect required, working around and from the basic shapes of the cube, cone, sphere and cylinder. A round shape is satisfying in its completeness and continuity. Triangular forms, based on the pyramid or cone, are among the most stable forms in art and nature, and suggest stability and permanence, especially when low and broad. Tall, slender triangular forms are more aspiring, leading the eye upward. An inverted pyramid shape, on the other hand, suggests instability. Rectangular forms usually imply what is strong and durable, and again, look stable and assured. An arrangement may be based on one or a combination of these forms, the dominant form providing the essential interpretation.

Forms can be geometrically precise or more free in form. Angular forms tend toward the rectangular or triangular. Curved forms can be geometrical like the sphere or free-form, or biomorphic like most of the organic aspects of nature—pears, squash, eggs, amoebas. These are the forms suggestive of life and growth, and have always inspired artists. They have been copied or abstracted by painters, sculptors and craftsmen through the ages— contemporary designers too, appreciate the ways in which these organic curves can be reproduced to vitalise their work.

Roughly speaking, plant material can be classed into three basic shapes:

Spike forms, like larkspur, delphinium, stock, gladiolus, bulrush, and so on.

Rounded forms, such as roses, dahlias, chrysanthemums, daisies. And the more indefinite shapes, like statice, gypsophila, shrubby flowers and leaves.

Spike, or tapering forms, as discussed when describing line, lead the eye smoothly to the outside of the design. Rounded forms hold the eye, and are placed, in conventional designing, at the point of greatest emphasis. Small, composite forms make logical fillers and are a transition from the spiky to the round forms. Monotony of form detracts from the unity of a design. The eye finds variation more satisfying, and differences of form enhance through contrast to the opposites in shape.

Fig. 38. A design in the shape of an inverted pyramid induces a soaring movement of great buoyancy.

Fig. 39. Eye-catching round forms contrasted by long curved forms.

52

Chapter 14

COLOUR

COLOUR IS the element in design which we most readily respond to. It attracts and interests us, perhaps because it concerns us daily in the home, in clothes. We are used to choosing and arranging colours. Colour affects the senses and feelings. Even people who are perhaps insensitive to disharmony in line or texture will often protest instantly at a strident colour scheme. Again, colour is so forceful that it can blind us to other aspects, even shortcomings of a design.

Many people have an instinctive colour sense, and many arrangers have a natural flair for using it well. A sense of colour cannot be taught, though it can be stimulated by observation, and understanding its various aspects. It is such a rich medium for visual expression and communication that it is an asset to be able to use it really well. By observing all the subtleties and variations of colour, one can learn to be more selective in its use—to be more experimental, instead of using only the more obvious or 'safe' combinations. Not that uncontrolled use is to be advocated; the skilful distribution of a few well chosen colours can be immensely more effective than too many used without restraint.

Colours in flower arranging come to us ready mixed. In plants, colour is determined by their chemical construction and the amount of light they reflect. Few flowers or leaves are one pure hue—a flower that looks red, yellow, or blue, will reveal traces of another colour. Many leaves have a tinge of yellow or blue in their green. Nature is a wonderful colourist, and it is easy to be inspired by her schemes. A wealth of information and guidance is yours from a walk in the garden. Take a flower, and study the colour harmony in petal, pistil or stamen, stem and leaf. Some of the colour combinations are a revelation and an inspiration. Study the massed effect of colour in the border and the effect of colours seen against other colours.

Colour is not a constant element, but is relative to other factors like light, and the proximity of other colours. A yellow arrangement will look a different yellow placed against a green drape, and a grey, or a black drape. A bright colour will look brighter next to a dull colour than by itself. A dark colour appears darker and a light colour lighter placed next to each other. So in an arrangement, a flower that is light, placed next to a dark leaf, will look lighter than when placed by a leaf or another flower which is lighter than itself.

The quality of a colour will vary tremendously with the type, quantity and source of light under which it is seen. Haven't we all, to our chagrin, found how different some colour schemes planned in daylight look by artificial lighting? The three qualities of colour are hue, value, and intensity.

Hue is the name of the colour, like blue, yellow, green. There are six main colours in the spectrum—yellow, orange, red, violet, blue, green, with many variations in between as one colour merges into the next. The painter's pigment is an approximation of the rainbow's hues, and these arranged in the same order on a circle of paper can be used as reference when studying colour. Three of the main hues are primary colours, and are red, blue and yellow. Secondary colours from a mixture of two primaries are:

Green—from blue and yellow
Orange—from red and yellow
Violet—from red and blue.

The 'in-between' colours, called tertiary, of which there are very many, range from yellow-green, blue-green, blue-violet, red-violet, red-orange, yellow-orange. Colours that are 'opposites', like yellow and violet, orange and blue, red and green, are called complementary colours—that is, a primary, and its opposite secondary. They 'oppose' each other in character. Yellow, red and orange are warm colours which advance towards the eye and are called advancing colours. Violet, blue and green are cool colours and they recede into the distance, so are receding colours. Colours next to each other—related hues—are known as analogous hues, like blue, violet-blue, violet.

Then there is the value of a colour. This is the degree of its lightness or darkness. The lighter values of a colour are known as tints, the darker values shades; the greyed version is a tone. With pigments this would be done by adding white for a lighter value, black for a darker, and grey (with black and white) for a greyed value. Pink is a tint or a light value of red. Maroon is a shade, or dark value of red; a 'muddy red' would be a tone or greyed version of red.

The third quality is intensity. This describes its degree of brightness or dullness. Scarlet is a red of high intensity. Pink can vary from a bright, clear pink, to one that is neutralised, or greyed like a rose-beige. Most yellows are bright, most violets are dull. So every colour can vary tremendously in hue, value, and intensity. Selecting and organising these in an arrangement will depend on the particular effect required. Generally speaking, warm colours are cheerful and conspicuous, cool colours are soothing and restful. Cool colours at the outline with warm colours at the centre, increase the three-dimensional quality of the design. Used together, opposites in colour intensify and accent each other. Red next to green appears redder than when alone. Direct colour contrasts can be rather harsh, the more subtle are the combinations of shades, tints and tones of complementaries. Monochromatic schemes in tints, shades and tones of one colour can often be improved by a touch of contrasting colour.

Because we tend to look first and longest at anything out of the ordinary, very high and very low values draw our attention. So extremes are usually concentrated towards the focus of the design. The more intense the colour, the greater its pulling power. Thus the brightest colours are usually reserved for areas of highest interest. Equality of hue, value and intensity is usually not as satisfying as an unequal distribution, with a greater emphasis somewhere for unity.

Since our feelings are strongly affected by colour, it is a powerful element in interpretation. Colour symbolism through long association is familiar to most people. Red with fire, yellow with the sun, green with meadows and large expanses of nature's panorama, blue with the sky, black with night, and so on. However, colour has the personal association too, and means different things to different people.

Now that we have discussed our working vocabulary, you will realise that we see none of the elements in isolation, but in relation to one another. Each element is dependent for effect on another element or elements. We cannot see colour without form, form without space, line without form. Designers use each element, not as separate aspects, but as essentially related components.

PART TWO

Chapter 15

ARRANGEMENTS WITH ACCESSORIES

FLOWER ARRANGEMENTS built up around a theme or idea are interesting and popular. To convey the right atmosphere or idea, and to further the interpretation, an item or items other than plant material is often included. This, in flower arranging terms, is called an accessory. It can be an ornament of any kind—figurine, plate, candle, or other man-made object, or natural items like stones, shells, fossils and so on. Used discriminately, these additions can look natural and convincing. Mishandled they add nothing of value or beauty to the design.

To be 'right', an accessory must give the impression of being a necessary part of the interpretation, to the extent that its removal would reduce the effectiveness of the story or idea. So often it is an obvious afterthought, not an essential working part of the composition. Think of the accessory as you would the plant material, so that it is a considered part of the design right from the beginning.

Planned this way, it is more likely to be in harmony with the style, mood, and character of the arrangement, and to be of the right scale, colour and texture with the rest of the items used. Disharmony is bound to occur when the accessory is at variance with any aspect of the other design units.

Another common error is in the placement of accessories. They are often seen, isolated from the main rhythm and direction of the design as a whole. There should be an easy sequence from one item to another, so that one views the composition as an integrated grouping, not as a series of separate objects with no link from one to the other. Placing items at different levels can often help. You can see the effect of this in some of the compositions in this chapter, where rhythm and flow of the design is enhanced by careful placements.

It is a mistake to use too many accessories in the belief that this increases the impact of the interpretation. It rarely does. Arrange-

Following pages:
Fig. 40. 'In pensive mood'. A tranquil theme with alder, catkins, hellebore, primrose, moss, stone and a bronze figure deep in thought.

Fig. 41. 'Motionless like silence listening to silence.'

59

Fig. 42. 'Spring'. A familiar theme in a naturalistic setting. 'Growing' in and around the old mellow bricks are arabis from the rockery, narcissus, daffodils, double tulips and cherry blossom. Two yellow birds complete a simple interpretation.

ments laden with accessories seldom hold one's attention for long, as the unity of the design is usually ruined by overstatement. A few well-chosen, subtly incorporated additions are far more likely to capture the imagination, and create an appealing composition. Nature-made accessories are generally easier to use than manufactured objects, since they associate naturally with plant material. But with thoughtful study many a cherished ornament can be happily combined with the right material.

Fig. 43. 'Still life.' A brown and grey pottery jug, dark matt brown pottery plates, a rosy apple, plum and green grapes, with a preserved fatsia leaf, proteas and a coarse rust coloured cloth for a further contrast of texture.

Fig. 44. Seascape.

Fig. 45. Landscape.

64

Chapter 16

ARRANGEMENTS USING WOOD

USED APPROPRIATELY, wood can make a meaningful contribution to design. So often though, wood is used without relevance to the character of the composition as a whole. It then becomes an odd addition rather than an integral part of the design. To further the artistic effect of the arrangement, it should be considered in relation to the other items—its line, form, colour or texture playing an appropriate role.

Naturally, a lot will depend on the nature and special characteristics of the wood. Perhaps distinctive texture is its major asset. Then this can be associated in harmony or contrast with the other items to increase the textural interest of the design.

Other pieces might add a more effective note through colour quality and can again harmonise with mellow hues of dried materials, or emphasise through contrast the brighter colours of fresh. An arresting line or form will dictate yet another usage. Pieces of spectacular form and line are often quite difficult to combine with other items—like the wood in Fig. 46. The arresting shape of this suggested a solo performance, as any additional material here would be superfluous. A suitable container that emphasised its abstract form and attractive texture was sufficient for a complete composition—a study in line and form.

The wood in Fig. 47 also has considerable sculptural beauty, which should be exploited. Here it is the main feature of the design, with the rest of the items promoting its special feature. Line and form are left clearly revealed, not smothered by additional plant material.

Wood need not always play a dominant role. It can—as with the wood in Fig. 48—form the framework that features other items. Here, several pieces are combined to make the outline/structure of the design. It is not the major feature here, as interest is focused more on the colour and texture of the flowers and sea fern. Never-

66

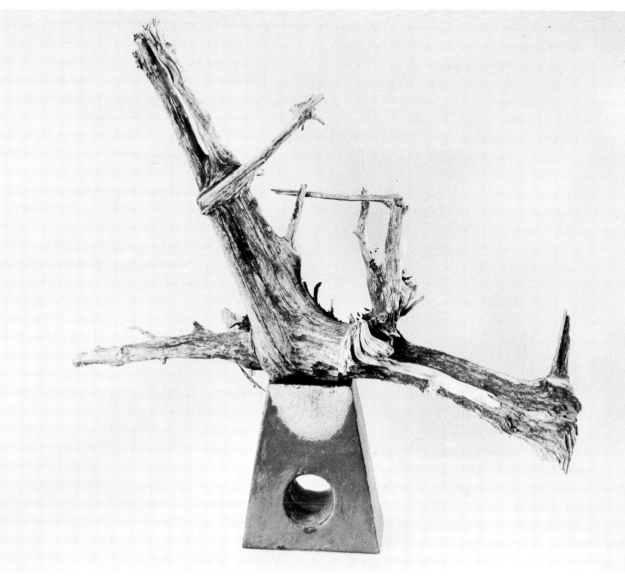

theless, the wood can be appreciated and seen, and it forms an
important part in the balance and rhythm of the design. It also
accents, through contrast, the texture of the coral.

Wood enhances the design quality of the arrangement in Fig. 49
also. By repeating the outline of the attractive wooden base, it
carries movement upwards. The rhythmical quality is thus further
promoted by the wood. Here too, through colour contrast, the
brilliant orange poppies are highlighted by the quiet tones of the
wood. Fig. 51 shows two pieces used for a whimsical theme.

Branches of tree ivy, wisteria and honeysuckle, if stripped when
freshly picked, then soaked in cold water, are easy to manipulate.
These can be curved into new shapes, tied until dry, and used in

Fig. 46. Wood; spectacular
enough to stand alone.

67

Fig. 47. Wood sculpture enhanced by the bold foliage and a container which complements its curves.

68

Fig. 48. Wood forms the outline of the design here.

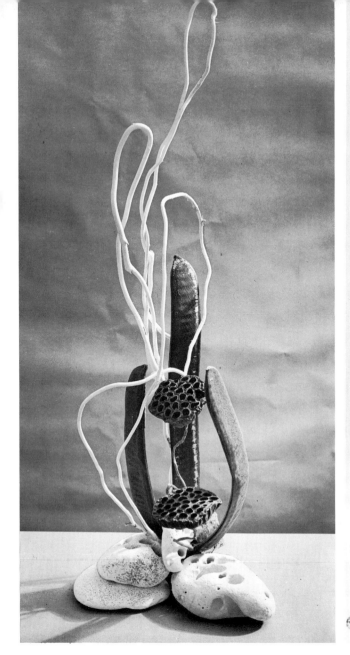

abstract and other designs. It is a good medium for enhancing spatial and linear effects and adding further interest in sparse arrangements. Such pieces are used in just that way in Fig. 50. These outline shapes were constructed from fresh tree ivy wood. Combined with giant seed-pods from the West Indies, they make an arresting space/form pattern for a design suggestive of modern sculpture, their malleability lending itself admirably to conveying this impression. You will find other examples of wood used in a non-realistic way elsewhere in the book.

Fig. 49. Wood used to add to the rhythmical quality of the design.

Fig. 50. An effect of modern linear sculpture with moulded ivy wood.

Fig. 51. 'Will you walk a little faster said a whiting to a snail; there's a porpoise close behind us and he's treading on my tail.'

71

Chapter 17

ARRANGEMENTS WITH DRIED AND PRESERVED PLANT MATERIAL

THE ARRANGER is constantly considering how to extend the possibilities in designing, and dried and preserved plant material certainly offer added scope. Without the need to have the stems in water, it is possible to design with greater liberty. The arranger too, is likely to feel less inhibited in bending, twisting, or altering the forms of the plants for a particular effect, than with living plant material. Exciting and original designs are therefore possible with this media.

This is evident enough at the major flower shows. 'Dried' classes no longer spell shapeless bundles of grasses, honesty, and sea-lavender, but distinctive, arresting arrangements. For whilst the dried has none of the light-reflecting quality of the fresh, it has other attractive features to commend its use. The sculptural quality of seedheads, interesting textures, and subtle, mellow colourings. In the home, too, they are eminently practical in centrally heated rooms. Each grouping far outlasts the time taken in construction— a boon for busy people, and a far more attractive proposition than the plastic counterparts.

The arranger's scope is now increased by the wide range of imported dried material. Initially a little expensive perhaps, but mainly so tough and durable, that it lasts indefinitely. Palmetto leaves, proteas in variety, banksia, lotus, cocos spathes, leucodendron and the like can add an exotic touch.

But with a little time and energy, marvellous things that cost nothing can be gathered from garden, field and hedgerow. With a little know-how, ordinary items—weeds even—can be transformed into ravishing beauties. For instance, dock or sorrel preserved instead of dried, looks positively exotic; poppy seed-heads turn a

steely blue with the same treatment. Or try preserving 'love-in-a-mist'—that delicate, filament-like foliage will remain intact. And if you leave aspidistra, or the leaves of iris foetidissima, molucella and atriplex in a sunny spot during the final stages of preserving, they turn a heavenly creamy-white.

You can get fascinating results too, if you take some items partly preserved, and hang them upside down. I have done this with ficus, fatsia and aspidistra leaves, so that there is a variation of green, tan, and brown, all in the one leaf. This is splendid for livening up an all-brown and beige arrangement. The stems of fatsia tend to soften in preserving. It is better to wire each leaf first, or to keep them firmly propped up.

I think it is more fun to be a little unconventional with one's methods. I try something different all the time, and preserve rather than dry, more and more as the result is so much more durable, and the material easier to handle. Dried items are brittle, but colour retention is so good in some things, dried in granular silica gel, that it is worth doing a little at least to add an interesting touch of colour to the dried. Small, bright red leaves of virginia creeper, or the fiery sumach; helleborus corsicus for that lovely soft green;

Fig. 52. A grouping of some favourite items; pampas grass, wild clematis, molucella, nicandra, achillea, teasels, leek seedheads, agapanthus, with leaves of aralia, *Mahonia bealei*, magnolia and laurel.

Fig. 53. The more exotic dried items; agave leaves, preserved strelitzia leaves and one protea.

73

Fig. 54. An arrangement stressing the sculptural beauty of dried material. Seed heads of agapanthus with dried aspidistra leaves are complemented by preserved iris foliage, and one palmetto leaf.

Fig. 55. Sculptured acanthus flowers, combined with two bold, intriguingly curved hosta leaves.

orange and yellow and red zinnias or some single pink roses. Gentle handling is needed in taking them out of the powder.

Skeletonising leaves is a rather laborious and messy process. It is possible to buy 'phantom' leaves fairly cheaply through flower clubs. You might care to experiment with bleaching broom though—it is a little less fragile to handle, and is rather useful for modern designs; it is also not cheap to buy bleached. Boil it for five minutes in a soda solution (roughly a tablespoonful to a pint), leave till cold, lay out on newspaper and strip off the fleshy part and then bleach if you want it even whiter, or dye for use at Christmas time. Teasle heads and fir cones are rather interesting bleached too.

74

The technique of drying

Drying can be done in three ways:

(a)—By hanging the items upside down in a cool, dry, airy place. This method is suitable for most seed-heads, grasses, cereals, and certain flowers like achillea, solidago, physalis, acanthus, larkspur, delphinium, liatris, amaranthus and others. 'Everlasting' flowers like helichrysum, acroclinium, rhodanthe, statice and xeranthemum are useful bright colour additions.

(b)—By pressing out moisture quickly with a cool iron, between layers of newspaper, or by laying the items to dry out more slowly, again between newspaper, weighted down. This produces a flat result and is suitable mainly for items like bracken and flat leaves that are difficult to preserve any other way.

(c)—With a preserving agent like borax or granular silica gel mixture—satisfactory chiefly with open-faced flowers like zinnia, marigold, sunflower, helleborus, single roses, dahlias—colour retention is good. The items do sometimes re-absorb moisture if left too long in a damp atmosphere. They can be re-dried by a short spell in the preservative—and then stored in an air-tight box with a few granules of the powder.

The technique of preserving

Certain plants may be preserved by immersing their stems in three or four inches of a solution made with one part glycerine to two parts of hot water until the material has completely changed colour. There is no shrinkage, and the result is pliable, workable, and durable, although the original colour of the plants is, of course, altered. Suitable subjects are the deciduous oak, beech, hornbeam, cotoneaster (salicifolia), sweet chestnut, and the evergreen laurel, *Mahonia aquifolium*, camellia, pittosporum and eucalyptus. Items like hosta leaves and hydrangea flowers can be left to dry naturally in a jar with an inch or two of water. Hydrangeas dry with better results when the plants are crisp to the touch.

General hints for successful drying and preserving

All items to be dried should be gathered during a dry spell. Flowers should be neither too young nor over-mature; when first nearing their perfection is best. Seedheads must be picked before they are too brittle, and if these are to be preserved rather than dried, then pick whilst they are still green. Leaves benefit by an initial drink in plain water. All woody stems should be crushed, and hot water used in the preserving solution. This should be thoroughly mixed, and the level watched and topped up when necessary. Cool, dry, airy conditions are essential, and a dark place for coloured items.

Chapter 18

ABSTRACT FLOWER ARRANGEMENTS

ABSTRACT ART is non-representational or non-realistic art. In abstract flower arrangement, we look at plant material in a new way, and use it to create new forms. To abstract is to simplify, by eliminating all extraneous detail, by separating the important from the unimportant, so that the essence or essential quality is represented, rather than the concrete detail.

In this experiment of using plant material differently, the aim is to create a form structure that suits the personal feelings for design, rather than conform to any set standard, as in traditional work. The aim is not to copy nature faithfully, though certain forms found in nature are often the source of inspiration—leaf-shaped voids, embryo-like shapes, patterns made by crossing, overlapping lines. It is discovering new shape and form patterns and developing these in more personal compositions.

A look at other art forms, such as painting and sculpture, and studying the history of art helps one to appreciate why artists of all times have used this process for communicating meaning. Ancient, primitive sculpture shows abstract quality in the distorted human form and grotesque faces of the gods. This was for symbolism and emotional impact rather than a stressing of abstract technique.

This quality in art has been further developed down the centuries as artists sought new ways to express their ideas, or to give greater emphasis to them. Cezanne, over a hundred years ago, ignored the mere surface appearance of objects, to stress their inner qualities, their solidity and weight. He observed that all natural items could be reduced to the sphere, the cone, and the cylinder. Van Gogh distorted or exaggerated hue and texture to intensify his expressions. Picasso did not paint an object like a violin as it appeared naturally, but with a strange medley of images which the eye relates one to the other in the painting. Kandinsky aimed to show painting as something complete in itself rather than a copy of

76

something in the natural world. Mondrian wanted to build up his pictures out of the simplest elements—straight lines and pure colours. He longed for an art of clarity and discipline that somehow expressed the fundamental rhythms in nature. His severe, architectural paintings bear no relation to anything familiar, their interest lies simply in the way space has been organised with line, shape and colour. Many abstract paintings seen to-day are this mere relationship of elements designed purely to entertain the eye. They are not meant to represent anything. They are not *about* something, but something in their own right. Other abstract paintings developed from a subject or theme are more expressive in style, termed abstract expressionism.

Much of modern sculpture too, shows the simplifying process of abstraction, and a new organisation of space. As in painting, the spaces left—the intervals between the forms—become as important as the forms themselves. Outer, and inner volumes allow the eye to see within and without simultaneously, not just the surface of the mass. Some forms are pierced, to increase the sense of depth in the sculpture. The sculptor has taken advantage of new materials, like plastic, wire and string, which give greater opportunities for defining space, and greater freedom in designing.

From these observations it can be assumed that abstraction is a means to an end—the means to personal expression without restriction. It seems logical for the flower arranger also to seek fresh ways of using plant material and to search for new techniques that give added opportunities to express ideas. All art, however, is conditioned to some degree by the nature of the medium used. Unlike the painter, or the sculptor, the flower arranger works with 'recognisable objects'—a flower is a flower, and a leaf is a leaf, however it is used. It could then be argued that it is not possible to create a purely abstract flower arrangement, if the theory that abstractionism rejects all recognisable things exists.

Would we really wish to do this to an extreme degree in flower arranging? Is the objective to establish a rigid style of non-objective character, with debates as to whether the various arrangements are or are not abstract, or is it more to expand the general scope of personal designing, with extensions compatible to our media?

The abstractionist arranger carries her work beyond the restrictions of traditional designing. It is a point of view, a way of seeing, an attitude which shows the trend to design beyond conventional boundaries, with the correspondingly unconventional and the freer usage of materials. It is not necessarily a more perfect way than the traditional, merely a freer one with a difference of interest.

The abstract character of an arrangement depends, in the main, on the use of the materials as design elements, in using their essential qualities for symbolism and expression. There will be degrees of abstraction—borderline designs, which embrace both traditional and abstract characteristics. Certain materials lend

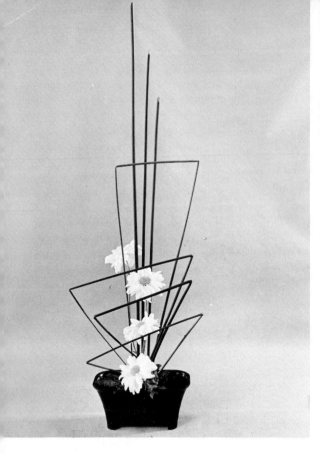

themselves more easily to non–realistic presentation because of their greater plasticity, and the tendency, increasingly perhaps in this sphere, will be to resort to that which has greater malleability.

Because of the great diversity possible, it is obviously difficult to classify abstract arrangements, but for discussion and clarification, as in other art forms, two broad, general groupings are possible—depending on the intent of the arranger.

One tendency is for compositions with no subject matter other than the design relationships. Examples are Figs. 56, 63, 66 and 67. In all these instances, the organisation of the different units of the design *is* the subject. They are simply patterns of lines that cut up space—there is no attempt to 'say' anything. Extra detail has been eliminated, and all is reduced to the essentials necessary to the design pattern. Fig. 56 is a design form, after the fashion of a Mondrian painting. It is severe and sharply geometric. Space has been used with a mathematical precision—the design is simple and disciplined.

Non-objective arrangements like these are not to everyone's liking. Some might say there is nothing to them, others agree perhaps with Matisse, that it is an 'art of balance of purity and serenity, devoid of any troubling subject matter'. Emotion, in the usual sense, is not communicated; the idea is to show things which are pleasing in their own right. Long ago, Plato said 'that straight

Fig. 56. The areas of space here are as rhythmical as the lines of movement made by the solid items.

Fig. 57. Stems of wild briar arranged into a lively pattern with black parrot tulips to accent the diagonal movement. The leaves and cut stalks create opposing movement and tension. The container repeats the general pattern of the design.

78

lines and curves, and the surfaces of solid forms produced out of these by laths and rulers and squares, are always beautiful'—with a beauty that is natural and absolute, in no way dependent on other things or the senses.

Again, as in the broader field of art, it is possible to make a second general classification in flower arranging, with designs drawn from a subject or a theme or idea. The subject is not always recognisable. By using the materials symbolically, the arranger conveys her sense impression of a scene, mood, object or experience. Examples of this type of abstract expression in the realm of sculpture are found in the famous bird and fish sculptures of Brancusi. One does not see the real bird or fish, but the form and movement of the sculpture suggests the inherent grace of fish and bird.

Figs. 57 and 58 show two abstract compositions developed from a theme/subject, though the image drawn may not coincide with the viewer's idea of the theme. Agreeing with the theme form should not really be the major concern of the viewer; the important appreciation is in the total form of the design. If the units are harmoniously assembled, one should be able to respond to the language of form and colour, and to enjoy the design relationships. Fig. 59 shows a realistic theme for comparison.

Fig. 58. Enter the serpent.

Fig. 59. A realistic rendering of a natural scene with iris flowers and foliage, reeds and lysichitum seed heads 'growing' out of the water. Stones and birds complete the theme.

The design characteristics

Since abstract arrangements are not constructed to any set plan, the units can be assembled in an infinite number of ways, but certain general features can be considered for clarification. It is interesting to compare the abstract with other types of design, remembering that there are no rigid, clear-cut divisions between one and the other.

In the traditional type of design, certain characteristics predominate. The plant material usually resembles the natural growth habit and plants are displayed to reveal their natural beauty. There is the conventional centre of interest, from which all stems radiate. The eye is drawn to this centre, where material is heaviest, and gently released through the transitional items to the outline of design by the finer, lighter material. Some of the items will be recessed for depth. There can be an interesting variety of form and texture, and the beauty is the beauty of mass. Fig. 60 shows an arrangement based on this style.

Figs. 61 and 62 are arrangements emphasising modern trends. Here, the design has a much sharper silhouette—line is accented, and there is a more planned and obvious use of space, so that the individual beauty of the plants is dramatised. Bold contrasts of form and texture replace profusion and greater variety of material. There is a breakaway from the massing of colour and texture, and an elimination of superfluous material. Apart from the odd trim-

Fig. 60. A traditional type design with arum lilies, white iris, single and double white tulips, *Helleborus corsicus* and *H. orientalis* with drooping sprays of *Garrya elliptica* in a gilded cupid container on a white marble base.

Fig. 61. A sparsity of material made more interesting by the sharp contrasts of the smooth solid surfaces of the lilies, arum leaf and clivia foliage, with the clipped palmetto leaves. The whiteness of the flowers is dramatised by the black metal structure.

Fig. 62. The beauty and interest of the plant material is left clearly revealed in this sparse modern arrangement.

ming and clipping of leaves, the material is still used realistically, placements are fairly conventional, and the area of greater interest still tends to be around the centre of the design.

In the abstract arrangements you will see that the items have been assembled quite differently. Here, the eye can begin its path anywhere; there is no static focal area. The eye is drawn from one interest area to another. No unit, no single part of an abstract arrangement is necessarily more important than any other. In this way, interest is equated over the entire design, rather than crowded into the central area. This you can see in all the examples given in this chapter.

Since the separate parts are not held together in the conventional centre, they are more isolated in space. Line does not always taper gently off as it moves to the outline of the design, as in traditional designing. Notice in Fig. 63 how the arrangement ends in a bold, eye-catching loop. The characteristic lack of transitional material strengthens the force of the design. However, the parts are all unified, and the structure of the design viewed as a whole. Each

Fig. 63. The rhythmical pattern of growth.

82

unit must be related to the other in a way that is easy to look at, and to make the design rhythmical. One should not be conscious of separate parts. Study the arrangements again to see how structural unity is maintained through careful placements, which give smooth eye movement throughout the entire design.

Space, of course, assumes great importance in abstract designing. Actually, the arranger models space with solids, so that it becomes a positive element. Space is used to tie together all the separate parts of the design through eye control. Space intervals speed up or slow down eye movement, depending on how close together they are. Space is very much part of the balance of the design. Notice how eye-catching the elliptical area of enclosed space is, made by the two lily stems in Fig. 64, and how it more than supports the weight of the solid leaves and flowers. The round areas, made by the palm strips looped together in Fig. 65 are equally dynamic and so are the spaces in the honeysuckle vines in

Fig. 64. The eye is drawn through the openness of this design by the gentle circular rhythms and pauses longest at the elliptical void formed by the two lily stems. The broad arum leaf, clipped iris foliage and loops of willow give contrasts in form. The circle and square described by the container give additional interesting shapes.

Fig. 65. Twirls of palm strips support the lively movement of three imported items.

Fig. 66. A study of line, form and space.

Fig. 63. Space, in abstract design, is not so much *in* the arrangement, as with traditional work, but *of* the arrangement.

Plant material is considered more in the role of design units, than for the part it plays in nature. Basically, material is line, form, texture and colour, so plant material is selected because of certain elements it possesses—the strength of a branch, roundness of a fruit, texture of a flower. Its quality is considered separately, and the natural is subordinated to the artistic purpose.

As the arranger is not concerned with representing realistically, plants are often altered or modified in appearance to increase their abstract quality. Strap leaves are often looped or clipped, part of a leaf used perhaps. Sometimes a flower stalk is used, with the bloom cut off. Dyeing or colouring items increases their abstract quality. Distortion is effective only when it adds to the beauty and expressiveness of the design, and distorting as a technique for commanding attention can result in a bizarre composition. Freedom from restrictions is necessary to allow the arranger full initiative to design imaginatively, but the aim is still to create a visually pleasing, aesthetically satisfying composition.

Fig. 67. Reeds used as lines enclosing space. The flowers are placed where they add to the three dimensionality of the design. The container repeats the angles of the design.

84

PART THREE

INTRODUCTION

THE FIRST parts of this book have been mainly instructional. I intend the last few chapters to be a sort of relaxation after hard work (for you and me!).

When there is a specific item to discuss, the arrangements must naturally be pre-planned to illustrate the relevant topic. Without this obligation one is more free to work around the inspiration itself, a more enjoyable and less limiting process. These few chapters therefore will be less deliberate in instruction, and designed more as a stimulation to your imagination and flights of fancy.

Chapter 19

INSPIRATION AND INTERPRETATION

WHEN THE basic principles of flower arrangement have been fully mastered, their use becomes more instinctive and their application less laborious. The arranger is then more free to work imaginatively. Creative arranging is exciting and rewarding, and the possibilities are without number.

Interpretive classes are ever popular at flower shows, and are a challenge to the imagination. In these instances, the competitor's interest is expected to be stimulated by the given title. This can be one which suggests a mood, a feeling, interprets the seasons, or a quotation to illustrate a topical theme, or tell a story. The knowledge acquired from the principles of designing will now guide the arranger to the most effective ways of communicating her ideas. She will consider and choose plant material, container, accessories perhaps, and the type of design and placements that best suit the interpretation.

Schedule makers have an obligation to the competitor, and should make the titles as stimulating as possible. Instead of the all too frequent, prosaic and mundane favourites like 'An arrangement in pastel colours', 'Shades and tones of one colour', why not an inspiring line that evokes some feeling and response, such as 'In the misty morn', 'When night is on the hills' and 'By moonlight, by candlelight, and by dreamlight', instead of 'An arrangement incorporating candles'? And who could fail to respond to such beautiful quotations as 'Have you but seen a fair lily grow', or 'A primrose by the river's brim'?

Not that they need all be of a nostalgic or romantic nature. Other moods, like humour, gaiety, excitement and so on can be evoked with appropriate titles too. The spark that gives the stimulus which is inspiration, can come from many sources evoked by innumerable things; a stirring piece of music, poetry, the ballet,

pictures or sculpture; sometimes from the simple things of everyday life:

'*White plates and cups, clean gleaming,*
Ringed with blue lines, and feathery faery dust
Wet, roofs beneath the lamplight.' (Rupert Brooke)

Most artists have found their greatest inspiration from the world of nature. The flower arranger works closer than any artist to this rich, inexhaustible source. Wonderful, varied Nature, with her storehouse of treasures, which speak eternally through the language of colour and shapes, light and shadow.

In plant life alone, the arranger's choice is endless—the velvet petals of a rose, the incredibly intricate pattern of Queen Anne's lace, the varied shapes of fruit, hoary lichen, and brilliant flowers. Or inspiration may come from nature's wider canvas—quiet waters, dew on the grass, the subtle mingling of cloud and mist on a rainy day, shadows in the evening light. The two arrangements in this

Fig. 68. 'In the bleak mid-winter'; a simple arrangement to depict a cold wintry scene.

Fig. 69. 'Now fades the last long streak of snow'—Tennyson; a nonrealistic interpretation of the title.

88

chapter were both inspired by a particular wintry scene, as I drove through the Plynlimmon Mountains in Wales.

Stony, craggy, infinitely sparse of vegetation, the hills stood cold and silent. Thin rivulets trickled to the stream below. It was a scene so bleak and desolate, yet the play of light and shadow made by the scurrying clouds, the odd, solitary tree etched against the sky, had a moving, poignant beauty. I have tried to convey these impressions in the arrangement in Fig. 68 with plant material, container, and accessories that create a bleak and wintry atmosphere. Sparse material, cold colours, an almost bare 'tree' all help to illustrate the theme.

The other composition (Fig. 69) is a re-creation in a different style of the same scene, as I saw it a few days later after the snow. A view still bare and almost leafless, but with the odd patch of white, here and there of the 'last long streak of snow' that so often lingers on the colder slopes after the thaw. Here again, textures, colours and placements help to reflect the nature of the scene and to interpret my impressions.

Inspiration is a strange, elusive thing. It does not always hasten to our beckoning, and often works in an unpredictable way. It is not something learnt from books, but comes from looking at all around us with an artist's delight, which enriches mind and imagination. Impressions stored in memory can be of inspiration later. The emotive, inspirational quality of an arrangement is what raises it from the mundane to the stimulating.

Chapter 20

THE DAFFODIL

IN SEEKING inspiration, the flower arranger need look no further than her material. The beauty of a flower, leaf, or twig can inspire creativity. The daffodil may not be the easiest flower to arrange. A characteristic stiffness and angularity makes it a difficult design subject, and the stems do not take kindly either to a pinholder or Oasis. Yet, it is a very appealing flower. It is at once bold and delicate, enduring and ephemeral, gay and wistful—qualities to inspire many differing expressions.

This is not my impression alone—the poets and the great writers have also felt this way about the daffodil. Shakespeare applauds its strong, enduring quality, in braving the rigours of winter, and appearing 'before the swallow dares', and yet 'takes the winds of March with beauty'. To him, they were the bright heralds of more pleasant days to come, for:

> 'When daffodils begin to peer,
> Why, then comes in the sweet o' the year.'

Robert Herrick though, considers more its ephemeral nature, and weeps to see it fade away so soon, long before the 'lasting day has run to even-song'. He wistfully compares this to man's equally brief span on earth, for:

> 'We have short time to stay—as you,
> We have as short a spring;
> As quick a growth to meet decay,
> As you or any thing.'

A sad contemplation indeed.

Tennyson too, feels that, 'when the face of night is fair on the dewy downs, the shining daffodil dies', though he has a more vigorous impression of the flower in 'a roaring moon of daffodil'.

Milton though, will have the flowers mourn, and:

'*Daffodillies fill their cups with tears*
To strew the laureate hearse where Lycid lies.'

But they arouse no sad thoughts for Wordsworth, whose heart danced with the daffodils. To him, they twinkled and outshone the stars, and so:

'*A poet could not but be gay*
In such a jocund company.'

What is more, he was able to recapture the joy in solitude through 'that inward eye'.

I imagine they all sang of the 'ordinary' woodland daffodil with 'a yellow petticoat, and a green gown'. Some of the modern beauties, are, of course, quite different—king-sized, paled to cream or pink, two-toned or with new exotic forms. These are all very lovely and look splendid in the more sophisticated groupings. But, to me, the 'true' daffodil is still the one that proudly bears its golden trumpet. Perhaps it is because I am Welsh and remember how we patriotically sported a yellow daffodil on St. David's Day at school (it was either that or a leek!). We could pick them from the fields, where they grew profusely in thick clusters, peeping from the grass, so that one came across them suddenly—'all at once', like the poet.

Fig. 70. '. . . Beneath the trees, fluttering and dancing in the breeze.'

Fig. 71. '. . . Daffodils that come before the swallow dares and take the winds of March with beauty.'

Fig. 72. '. . . They flash upon that inward eye which is the bliss of solitude.'

92

Chapter 21

THE EMPTY SPACES

INSPIRATION does not always come from the visible or the tangible. It can be prompted from many other sources, sometimes quite unexpectedly. I was looking for a book at the library, when I chanced upon *The Empty Spaces*, a collection of poems by Sarah Churchill. I enjoyed reading these very beautiful, poignant poems, but it was the title itself that caught my imagination and provided the inspiration for the arrangements in this chapter.

More correctly, it was the philosophy from which the title is derived. This originates from the morality of an ancient Chinese work, the Tao-Te-Ching, which maintains that 'we turn clay to make a vessel, but it is on the space where there is nothing that the utility of the vessel depends. Therefore, just as we take advantage of what is, we should recognise the utility of what is not.' A truth and sentiment, admirably expressed as only sages can, and a philosophy that applies to art also. For here too, we use 'what is', but appreciate the function of 'what is not'.

In flower arrangement we utilise plant material to make a beautiful arrangement, but recognise the value of the unfilled areas in enhancing this. It is the empty spaces that give meaning to the solid items, just as the objects themselves are needed to delineate, and give significance to space.

We are now familiar with the effects of space in arrangement and how it can improve a design. I have discussed space as an element and how it is used in flower arranging in Chapter 12. In the context of inspiration, it is more relevant to discuss the aesthetic implication of space in art. Empty areas have a quieting effect on the senses. Just as the margins of blank spaces on the printed page rest the eye and make the print easier to read, so the surrounding space makes form easier to see and appreciate in an arrangement. We respond to the order and harmony of a well spaced composition, just as we are bothered and flustered by an overcrowded one, whether it is a flower arrangement, painting or living room. Gardens too, are compositions where we try to create a sense of space. It would seem

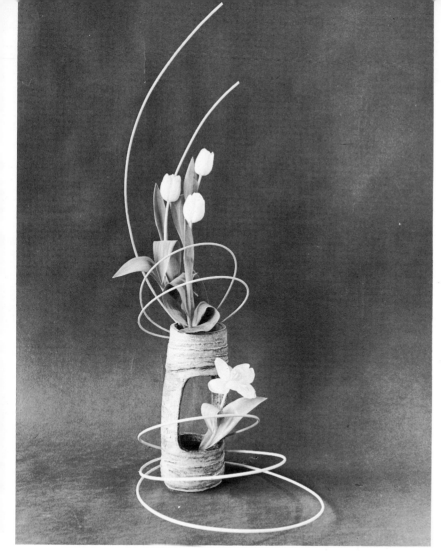

then that we need space for spiritual satisfaction.

Space lends a touch of mystery, since it invites the imagination to fill in the details of the empty areas. Consider the effect on the eye and mind of a relatively empty landscape, or one clothed in newly fallen snow. Comparable too, in art, is the effect of a large empty area, deliberately left bare, but which is very much part of the picture as often seen in a Japanese painting. Empty spaces in arrangement encourage this imagining too. One can invent from 'what is not'. When all is visible or obvious all at once, there is no subtlety, nothing to ponder on, no mystery. Space then can lead to contemplation.

On the other hand, space can give more vigour and mobility to a design, since it ties together all the separate parts. With space between the solid items, the eye can explore all the interesting facets of the material, all the variations in the structure of the design. This adds to the depth and mobility of the arrangement. And when space is used with as much importance as the solid

Fig. 73. Here the spaces are as positive as the solids and create such verve and movement that the items seem almost to be moving.

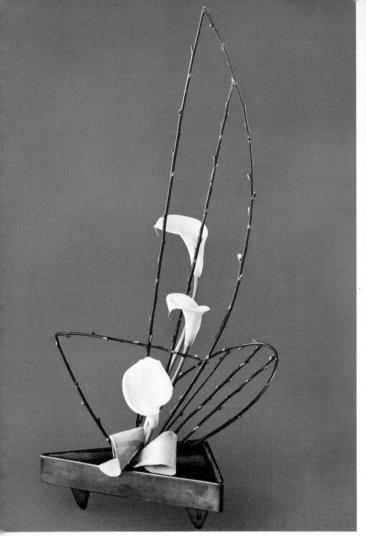

Fig. 74. The eye is drawn to the sculptural beauty of the lilies, but wanders also to the interesting shapes of the empty spaces.

Fig. 75. Space brings added depth to this design so that we seem to view the flowers from a distance.

objects, it is obvious that the interest of the viewer will alternate from one to the other.

Sometimes the plant material will command most attention—at other times, the beauty of the voids. This increased eye-pull gives greater verve and expressiveness to an arrangement than one where space is deemed of little importance. Space has meaning and energy. Clearly the two elements of space and solid gain emphasis and significance through their mutual differences. Space is needed in which to see objects, and objects are needed to define space. We appreciate the qualities of one through contrast with the other.

In the same way that the sound of music is enhanced by its pauses of rest and an actor pauses for dramatic effect, or to give greater significance to words, the artist with plant material emphasises the beauty of a flower by framing it in space. We become more aware of the special qualities of the flower, but realise too, the contribution of space in this enhancement. Which brings me back to the philosophy of the sage of long ago—the recognition of the value of 'what is not'.

Chapter 22

SCULPTURE IN WOOD

WOOD HAS A special fascination for the flower arranger, and is often the inspiration for a floral composition. But to present its most arresting aspects and bring out the intrinsic qualities of the wood, the arranger must use it discriminately, and be selective in choosing the additional plant material.

The special features of the wood can be the initial guide. This might be an interesting texture, a wonderful colour perhaps, dramatic line or arresting form. Or it might have several outstanding features, to suggest different presentations, and so give variable effects, like the wood pictured here—Fig. 76. It has many attractive features, which have inspired quite different interpretations. I hope to discover yet more assets, and add to the pleasure of its use. It is a slice of tree trunk, mounted on a matching base, and has an interesting range of textures. It is also a rich, pleasing colour which varies from dark to light brown. Its dimensions are also quite a challenge.

But I feel that the strongest appeal is its wonderful line and form, its superbly structural quality. Indeed it is complete as a piece of wood sculpture, reminding one of the classical, timeless beauty and order found in a Barbara Hepworth sculpture, or the vitality and massiveness of a Henry Moore masterpiece. These impressions vary with the position and angle of the wood. I found it suggested a different image from each viewpoint. These I have tried to interpret in the different compositions.

In the one view (Fig. 77) a vivid, three-dimensional aspect is created by the variations in the planes of the wood and the shadows it creates. This gives an awareness of depth and hollows and a tunnel-like perspective. It is easy to imagine a cave. There is a certain mystery and a little of the fascination felt in looking at a cavern in the hillside. It was this aspect of the wood I felt had a suggestion of the repose and ponderous quality of a Moore sculpture. Or does it suggest to you a breaking wave? The white flowers can be the riding surf that shifts and dashes the pebbles on the shore.

97

Or perhaps it is a bud uncoiling—'The awakening' or 'The beginning'.

To leave the imagination free to choose the personal interpretation I did not want to augment too heavily with extra material, and the wood itself conveys enough. The plant material and accessory, therefore—if you accept the first interpretation—merely accent the effect of light and shadow, stress the sense of depth and repeat the line and sculptural form of the wood.

In Fig. 79 the wood is at a similar angle, but turned to the reverse side. The convexities and concavities of the wood are now seen at a more rhythmical angle, effecting greater movement and linear beauty. I felt nothing should reduce this rhythm and strong spatial interest—an abstract design with dried reeds seemed to accent these special features. This was inspired by certain Hepworth sculptures where she combines string or wires with a solid form, giving a sensation of spaciousness and clarity and rhythmical spatial beauty. Movement goes out from the solid form to space

Fig. 76. The basic material, a slice of hollow tree trunk mounted on a matching base, is in itself a work of art with an interesting range of textures, shapes and colours.

Fig. 77. Is it a cavern or a sweeping wave rolling towards the shore? Your own imagination can probably provide many interpretations of this arrangement.

Fig. 78. A nook for contemplation, setting the mood for a realistic scene.

Fig. 79. An abstract design with great movement and linear beauty. The dried reeds seem to accent these special features.

and from space inwards to the object. I have tried for a similar effect here with plant material.

In yet another position (Fig. 78) the wood forms a nook for contemplation and sets the mood for a realistic scene. In this different role the line of the wood is more encompassed and fused into that of the plant material. But this does not lessen the impact of line and form, seen again from quite a different angle.

100

Chapter 23

MOODS FOR MEDITATION

THERE IS something almost magical about art, for the artist somehow achieves what would seem impossible. A sculptor, for instance takes shapeless, lifeless matter like stone or clay and moulds or carves it into a recognisable form, sometimes quite incredibly full of life and movement. On a perfectly flat surface the painter can give an illusion of depth and distance and with just a few tubes of paint can create a picture that speaks volumes.

There is this same magic in flower arranging. Here so much can be said, and so very eloquently, with plant material. The arranger can also express ideas, capture a mood or tell a story as effectively as the painter or sculptor or artists with other media. Flowers, of course, are neither lifeless nor shapeless, but creatures with a distinctive personality. It needs the arranger's skill—the magic wand—to fully reveal their intrinsic qualities and to use these for interpretation.

The effectiveness of the expression will depend on the right choice of material, and on the organisation of the different elements that best portray the theme. In each of the arrangements in this chapter, I have tried to convey a particular mood, suitable to the quotation which inspired it.

The first of these (Fig. 80) has an air of tranquillity. A small boat at rest, in a quiet cove perhaps, shaded by trees, cool, white flowers, water loving plants and grasses swaying lightly in the breeze, convey the quiet, lonely pool. Perhaps a kingfisher will come along as in the poem to seek this solitude. The casual design, cool colours and suitable accessories all help to create a tranquil feeling.

A mood of contemplation is suggested in the next arrangement (Fig. 81). The old man sits quietly by the still waters with his pipe and his thoughts. He does not look particularly prosperous in the material sense, but is perhaps rich with the wisdom of age. Maybe he realises the value of a serene mind, and a few quiet moments to contemplate. Here too, the type of design and the items used suit the theme and convey the particular mood of the quotation.

Fig. 80. 'A quiet place, a lonely pool.'—W. H. Davies.

Fig. 81. 'Give me, kind Heaven, a private station, a mind serene for contemplation.'—John Gay.

By the same principles, a very different feeling is created in the third arrangement (Fig. 82). Here, the plant material is spiky and prickly, with the major lines of the design harsh and forceful. This is a turbulent mood. There is the threat of someone's anger, or cruel forces ready to engulf and trap. The flowers seem to ask which way points to escape out of this turmoil. Fig. 83 takes on a mood of fatalism. It speaks of resignation as one ponders on the

inevitable. Life is beautiful, but brief, like a lovely, fragile bloom with little time from bud to flower, and so very soon the petals fall. Life's journey is often perilous, through devious and uncertain paths.

Perhaps you would have liked much gayer and more humorous moods, but these seemed rather apt for meditation and are what the moment's inspiration yielded. Who knows what the next may be, or from what source? That is part of the magic too.

Fig. 82. 'Which way shall I fly, infinite wrath and infinite despair?'—Milton.

Fig. 83. 'Stop and consider; life is but a day, a fragile dewdrop on its perilous way.'—Keats.

Chapter 24

INSPIRATION FROM THE BIBLE

W ELL CHOSEN words inspire the imagination and set the mood for creativity. For sheer poetry and superb expressiveness, there are few to equal those of the Bible. Everything is told superlatively, and though it would be difficult to interpret some of its philosophy and statements through the medium of flower arranging, there are many themes and ideas throughout that lend themselves to effective interpretation.

One need go no further than the first chapter of the book of Genesis to find a whole range of splendid suggestions. Indeed, the first three verses alone are full of inspiration. In fact, the 'Days of creation' would be a terrific show theme, with classes like, 'In the beginning', 'Let there be light', 'The face of the water', 'The earth, and the herb-beating seed', 'The sun, moon, and stars', 'The winged fowl that fly', and 'The beasts of the earth'.

Or, an equally interesting and varied schedule could be built around the chapters that follow which tell of the creation and the fall of man. It could include such themes as 'The garden of Eden', 'The tree of knowledge—of good and evil' or 'Enter the serpent'— a popular one without doubt.

Then there are those best remembered themes in the Old Testament of Noah and the Ark, of Cain and Abel, Lot's wife, Ruth the gleaner, Samson and Delilah, the Queen of Sheba—who came 'with camels that bore spices, and very much gold and precious stones to King Solomon who exceeded all the kings of the earth for riches'. And there is the theme of Moses (the ark of bulrushes hidden in the flags of the river bank, and later the flame of fire and the burning bush).

There are so many more—from the New Testament also. From the miracles we have 'The stilling of the tempest', 'Healing of the leper', 'Feeding the five thousand (loaves and fishes)', 'Lazarus raised from the dead', and 'The wedding in Cana (turning the

water into wine)'. There is 'The nativity', 'The last supper', 'The betrayal', 'The crucifixion', 'The empty tomb', 'The resurrection and the ascension', and 'Palm Sunday'. Inspiring themes there, told with an eloquence that challenges the imagination. Age-old themes that can be interpreted in any manner or style. I have chosen to do so in the modern idiom, but any number of ways would be equally effective.

It is easy to be inspired by the psalms, they are so uplifting. 'The

Fig. 84. 'In the beginning.'

Fig. 85. 'Let there be light.'

105

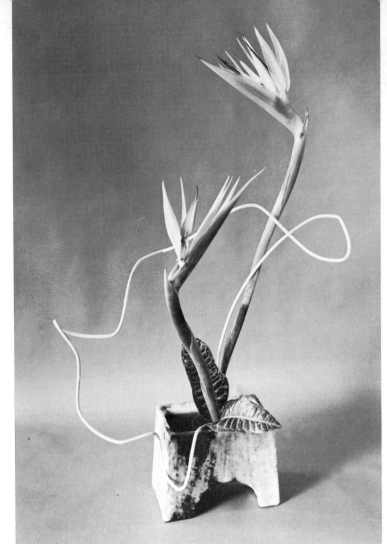

heavens declare the glory of God', 'The Lord is my rock and my fortress', 'I will lift up mine eyes unto the hills', 'The work of thy fingers, the moon and the stars', 'Out of the depths have I cried unto thee, O Lord', 'He leadeth me beside the still waters', and the whole of the 23rd Psalm.

There are many well expressed thoughts and ideas elsewhere which inspire through the music of words. For instance: 'They shall mount up with wings as eagles', 'The voice of him that crieth in the wilderness' and 'The heavens shall vanish away like smoke, and the earth shall wax old like a garment'. And two verses from the second book of Samuel—my own special favourites. One for the entrancing image it evokes, 'He rode upon a cherub, and did fly, and he was seen upon the wings of the wind'. And the other for its exquisite beauty of expression, 'And he shall be as the light of the morning, when the sun riseth, even a morning without clouds, as the tender grass springing out of the earth by clear shining after rain'.

Fig. 86. 'Above the Earth (in the open firmament of Heaven).'

Fig. 87. 'Consider the lilies.'

106

Chapter 25

CULINARY COMPOSITIONS

MY INSPIRATION this time comes from a very familiar and homely source—the kitchen. Like most housewives this is where I spend an enormous part of my life. It is heartening therefore, to find something that inspires creativity in such surroundings and in the tasks involved. In particular, that of preparing food—a chore of most constant recurrence.

To the receptive, inspiration can come from various quarters—the food itself, the gadgets or any of the attractive paraphernalia used in preparations. The most obvious to the flower arranger/cook is from the 'natural plant material' section. To this we are dedicated so it is easy to be rapturous over a cauliflower or a cabbage, to find a bunch of carrots alluring, or to see the terrific design potential in sticks of rhubarb. A turnip makes a fine centre of interest; celery and leeks are good outline material, parsley, mint, and thyme are excellent for transition. Indeed, the fruit and vegetable kingdom has all the variety needed for a good design used alone or of course, combined with other plant material.

First of all, the choice of shapes. There are simple, basic rounds, ovals and cones, as well as an abundance of free form, exciting shapes. Then there is a wealth of textures to give variety and contrast—shiny, smooth peppers and aubergines, velvety matt peaches, pitted surfaces like oranges, and the rough fascinating textures of pineapple, melon, Chinese gooseberries and certain varieties of avocado pear. A look at some of the Dutch 17th century still-life paintings proves how attractive and inspiring the surface textures are. The artists have managed to convey the deliciously mouth-watering quality of the different fruits painted.

And there is plenty of colour too, from vivid brilliant primary colours to subtle tones and shades; the vegetable grouping (Fig. 89) is very colourful. Orange carrots and the brighter orange-red capsicums, pimentoes and tomatoes, contrasted by the pale and dark greens of the celery and courgettes. To prevent a flat and solid look, accents of white were carefully placed to add depth and movement

by the effect of light and shadow thus created. The casserole is bright orange—a splendid boost to morale and appetite, these gay, modern crocks. The clean line of the wooden spoon is attractive too, it breaks up the roundness of the pot and strengthens structural harmony.

The glasses and the wine decanter (Fig. 90) have very pleasing shapes as well. Suitably placed they make a rhythmic addition to the design. Even the cheese cutter is an important linear element here, and the foliage, fruit and food combine through pleasant association to make an appropriate composition.

Onions are of course quite beautiful, their texture most pleasing and forms varied and interesting. In Fig. 91 at their varying stages

Fig. 88. Tribute to a melon.

Fig. 89. One for the pot.

108

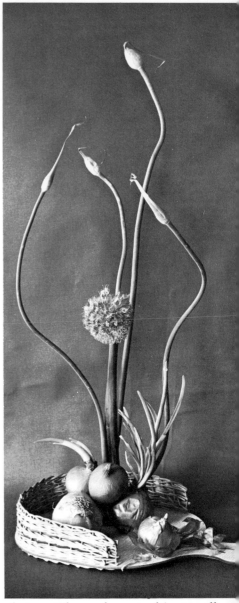

of growth they make a complete design. The melon combines well in colour and texture with sansevieria and a yellowing fatsia leaf for a modern composition to smarten up my kitchen and to remind me that I am a flower arranger.

But I must return now to my cooking. The preparation and the presentation of food primarily satisfies an important basic need, but like flower arranging it is also a spendid artistic outlet. Perhaps the flower arranger ought to bear in mind which she is indulging in at any one time. Beware of all-green or all-white meals, or even worse, slices of sansevieria in the salad!

Fig. 90. Cheese and wine.

Fig. 91. A family of onions.

110

Chapter 26

THEMES FOR EASTER

THE EASTER festival has many different aspects. It has a deep religious significance, and again a more light-hearted vein. Easter arrangements are as much a ritual and a tradition for the church as at Christmas time, though we do not perhaps decorate our homes with quite the same seasonal fervour, or on quite the same scale.

But the keen flower arranger is invariably involved in exhibiting at the first spring shows, where Easter interpretations are likely to be included in the schedule. These offer great scope for variety and unlike Christmas, Easter is at a time of year when plant material is more plentiful and varied. Branches with buds bursting into leaf, fresh green leaves from the garden and hedgerow and colourful spring flowers make the range of interpretation greater than when everything is scarce and expensive.

A large number of the Christmas decorations rely heavily on the painted or glittered and artificial. Easter compositions are predominantly fresh and natural. The white and gold or pastel hues of spring are so refreshing. Arrangements can vary from the gay and light-hearted—the Easter bonnet, Easter parade, arrangements including Easter gifts, fun arrangements with birds and bunnies and pretty groupings for our Easter table—to interpreting the deeper meaning of Easter.

Of the arrangements in this chapter, two are in lighter and two in a more serious mood. The one with the baby chicks (Fig. 92) would appeal to the children or could be used as a pretty arrangement for the home. Two of these fluffy charmers are yellow, the other three a pale mauve and they have just emerged from a king-size golden egg. The mimosa suits their texture and colour, while the curvy outline material of the setsuka willow matches the line and colour of the polished wooden base. I know the mimosa will not stay fluffy for long but its fragrance lingers for ages and it is very pretty even when it shrinks.

The second grouping (Fig. 93) is a fantasy, the product of my imagination. The pottery hen (her name is Matilda) is a soft blue-

grey and matt textured. She sits on a 'nest' (modern version) of the same colour. Plant material here is used in a non-realistic way. The outline of dried bamboo has been trimmed into neat tufts. Strips of soft wire, painted white, are complemented on the other side by a strip of palm, 'teased' out to resemble straw. Using the eggs made me realise what an attractive form and texture they have, and they are, of course, suitably symbolic for Easter.

The other two arrangements have a religious theme, one in sharp contrast to the other. Plant material, and the nature of the design in each instance, give the appropriate expression to the two interpretations so that a different emotion is conveyed in each. In the one theme, the flowers and the main lines of the design droop downwards. The rough, prickly textures, sharp lines and pointed

Fig. 92. Fun and frolics.

Fig. 93. A festive fantasy.

Fig. 94. The sorrow of Good Friday; '. . . He died on the cross'.

112

forms symbolise the suffering on the cross. The red flowers strengthen the interpretation.

In the other composition the lines of movement lead the eye upward, with the flowers arranged in an ascending vertical pattern to signify the glory of the resurrection. Textures here are smoother, forms more rounded and the outline of the design is softer. The white lilies are symbolic of the purity of the risen Christ.

These are some of the themes for Easter—there are very many more. We shall enjoy the contrast and the variety at home, at the shows, and also in church.

Fig. 95. The joy of Easter day; 'Rejoice for He hath arisen'.

Chapter 27

THEMES FOR CHRISTMAS

EACH SEASON of the year has its different highlights for the flower arranger. Spring, summer, autumn and winter bring their own special inspiration. With the glory of the garden a mere memory, winter might well hold the bleakest arranging prospects, were it not for Christmas. Addison quotes Sir Roger de Coverley, shrewdly observing that 'It happens very well that Christmas should fall out in the middle of winter'.

This festive season affords the enthusiast scope for greater diversity of arrangements than at any other time, and there are many sources of inspiration to stimulate the imagination. The many aspects of winter itself are inspiring, and easy to interpret. Bare branches seen against the winter sky, the sky itself tinged with crimson when the sun goes down on a clear, frosty day. The contrast of bright red berries against the sombre greens, shimmering, frosted branches that look like enchanted trees. Or inspiration may come from all the sparkle and glitter of the shop window, or the bigger decorations of illuminated splendour in towns and cities, and mammoth Christmas trees, trembling and shimmering under their load of coloured baubles.

With painting, dyeing, and glittering a permissible clause in the Christmas schedule, the arranger can make the most dazzling creations, and in the most scintillating and unusual colour schemes. Even schedule makers can lose their inhibitions, and give the competitor every chance to be daring and original. It gives the judge a break too! So Christmas shows, bewitching in sparkle and colour, are immensely popular with one and all.

The many other aspects of Christmas can be interpreted also. The different facets of its celebration. An eat, drink, and be merry time, party-time and conviviality. Gift-time, with mysterious parcels done up in gorgeous wrappings; exquisitely decorated, special dinner table centre-pieces, and coloured candles.

Then there are the many legends associated with the festival, from all times and countries. One of the best known is the legend of the

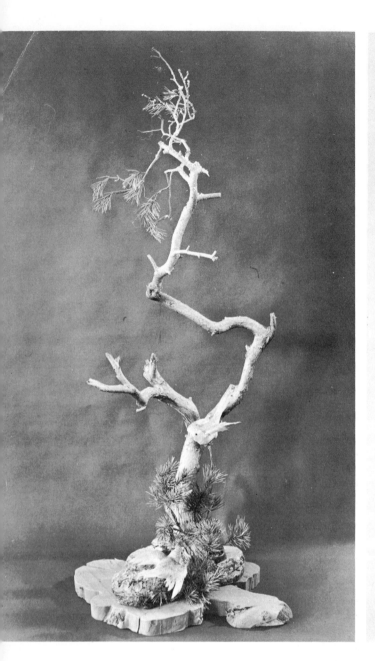

poinsettia—touching in its story of the poor peasant child anxious to present a token of his love and devotion, but with no money for a lavish gift. His roadside weeds were transformed into the most brilliant blooms. The new improved varieties of the poinsettia make a most practical cut flower because of its splendid lasting qualities. The green leaves might tend to drop after a while, but the vivid scarlet bracts last for ages, and they are an excellent contrast to the greenery, and look wonderful with variegated holly.

Fig. 96. A Winter's Tale.

Fig. 97. The legend of the poinsettia.

116

Fig. 98. Eat, drink and be merry.

The carols, with their wide choice of themes, inspire by the beauty of the images they evoke. The Christmas story itself has tremendous inspirational appeal. This age-old theme can be told—in the flower arranger's language—in many different ways. This can be a realistic manner, with the familiar figures of the Nativity, which tell the story simply and directly in a traditional, or a modern design, with fresh material, or the glittered. Or the theme can be expressed in a non-realistic way, which is more subtle, and perhaps more challenging.

The annual repetition of the Christmas decorations and interpretations seem in no way to blunt the enthusiasm of arrangers everywhere and new, exciting presentations seem to emerge each year to surprise and delight us.

Fig. 99. Mother and Child.